PRESTON GRAMMAR SCHOOL

The History of Preston Grammar School

JAMES R. M. HEPPELL

Carnegie Publishing, 1996

The History of Preston Grammar School
by James R. M. Heppell

Published by Carnegie Publishing
18 Maynard Street, Preston PR2 2AL, Lancashire

Copyright © James R. M. Heppell, 1996

First edition, August 1996

ISBN 1-85936-036-X

British Library Cataloguing-in-Publication Data
A catalogue record for this book is available from the British Library

Typeset by Carnegie Publishing
Printed by Cambridge University Press

Contents

This book is dedicated to
'. . . the men who were boys when I was a boy'.

Introduction

Preston grammar school ceased to exist in 1969, and no full history of the School has hitherto been written. On 23 February 1995 the President of the Preston Grammar School Association presented to the Right Worshipful the Mayor of Preston a bound set of the School Magazine – the 'Hoghtonian', so that it might be deposited in the Preston Reference Library. This was done as a memorial to Ernest Walters who had been, prior to his death, a member of the Association for over 60 years. As mentioned hereafter he had deposited his own collection of Hoghtonians in the Library, and the set had been completed, and handsomely bound at the expense of the Association. During a conversation after the presentation ceremony it was suggested that I should write a history of the School, and this book is the result.

It has been produced with the full co-operation of the Association. I am responsible for the text, but the arrangements for the publication, and the collection of illustrations have been the responsibility of H. W. L. Cumming, without whose enthusiasm and dedication to the project it would never have succeeded.

I should like to thank the Libraries I have used – the Liverpool Athenaeum, Sefton Public Libraries, the Lancashire County Record Office, and the Preston Reference Library; Stephen Sartin and Ian B. Hoyle for answering my questions; the daughters of Norman Hodgson, Miss Isobel Hodgson and Mrs Christine Millest for information about their father; my wife for spending long hours transcribing parts of the manuscript minutes of the Borough Council and its Committees, and assisting in the correction of proofs; my daughter-in-law, Mrs Jill Heppell M.Phil., B.Sc., for carefully reading the original draft, and making corrections and comments; Alan Davies (former Principal of the Preston College) for similarly reading the draft; and the members of the Council of the Association who also read the draft, and gave me great assistance by providing information and documents.

Chapter 1

The Early Medieval Period

IT IS ONLY IN COMPARATIVELY RECENT TIMES that the early history of English Grammar Schools has been studied. The subject was little understood in the last century. A. F. Leach in his book *The Schools of Medieval England*, published in 1915, stated that few guessed, and fewer knew that there were any grammar schools, except Winchester and Eton, before the time of the Tudors. It was known that there were monastic schools where singing, and a little Latin were taught, but Furnivall in 1892 had categorically stated that there were no grammar schools before Edward VI. The Headmaster of a large Midland school (who incidentally believed, quite erroneously, that Alfred the Great founded Oxford University), asked about the history of his school, and could not believe that it probably dated back to the reign of Edward the Confessor. It is now difficult to understand this ignorance of the early history of education, since it is obvious that the students at Oxford and Cambridge must have received their early training somewhere.

Whatever schools existed in Roman Britain were swept away at the time of the Anglo-Saxon invasions, but when Saint Augustine brought Christianity to Kent in 597, it was necessary to establish a system for the training of priests, and the necessary preliminary to this would be instruction in Latin. He therefore established a school at Canterbury, probably in 598, and the present King's School has descended from it. Other schools were established elsewhere, and Alfred the Great could, during his war with the Danes, express the hope that 'If we have peace all the free-born youth of England, who are wealthy enough, shall be set to learning.'

In the reign of his son, Edward the Elder, a school was founded at Warwick, and as new boroughs were created, as a barrier against the Danelaw, grammar schools were founded in them.

Following the Norman Conquest, and the disturbances that ensued, further schools were founded which were of six types, namely: cathedral schools; monastery schools; collegiate schools attached to collegiate churches; schools attached to hospitals for the poor; guild schools organised by local trade guilds; and, later, chantry schools.

In Lancashire the oldest grammar school was probably that at Lancaster, founded about 1200. Preston followed shortly after, and then Middleton (probably in 1265, and certainly by 1412). In a town of importance it was obviously desirable that a school should exist, since the growth of trade would necessitate a certain level of literacy, and numeracy among the Burgesses. If there was no ecclesiastical school available it was for the guilds, in collaboration with the Corporation, to see that a school was provided, and this would involve the help of the Church.

In Preston, which had strong guilds from an early date, and a Guild Merchant from before 1179, it is most likely that a grammar school was founded, at least as early as the first part of the thirteenth century, but the date cannot now be ascertained. Having regard to the close relationship between the Corporation and the Guild Merchant, it was probably a joint foundation.

In the *Cartulary* of Cockersands Abbey eleven undated charters are listed, which were probably made in 1230. They all grant pieces of land in Preston to 'Magister' Willelm de Kirkham. The title magister would, at that time, denote that he was a graduate of a University, and it has been suggested by Leach that he was Master of the Grammar School, and that the lands were transferred to him as an endowment for the School. This is, to an extent, confirmed by the fact that, in some of the charters, it is recorded that the transfers of land were with the common assent of the whole town, the Burgesses confirming this by affixing the Common Seal. It is also interesting to note that some years later Thomas de Kirkham was appointed 'Schole-master' of Lancaster Grammar School. He was possibly the son of Willelm, and was not a priest because he had a wife called Emma.

The next reference to a Schoolmaster in Preston is in 1358. There was in Preston a leper hospital to which was attached a chapel dedicated to Saint Mary Magdalene. It was situated near where Saint Walburgh's Church now stands, and the district known as Maudland takes its name from the chapel. The hospital and chapel were founded during the reign of Henry II (1154–89) by a charter which is undated. It enjoyed the unique distinction, in Lanca-shire, of not being under the control of the Parish Church, or even of the Archdiocese. In 1355 Henry, Duke of Lancaster, obtained from the Pope a relaxation of one year and forty days penance for all penitents who visited the chapel on the principal feasts of the year, and on the feasts of Saint Mary Magdalene, and Saint Thomas of Canterbury.

On Monday 24 June 1353 a man named Nicholas Starkie murdered Richard Breton. He was not hanged, so he was probably in Holy Orders, and he managed to obtain a pardon from the Prince of Wales (the Black Prince) by Letters Patent dated 6 June 1357. On 3 May 1358, being the day after the feast of the Invention of the Cross, while a pilgrimage was taking place at the chapel, a proclamation of the pardon granted to Starkie was made. At that moment a large number of 'evil disposed persons' rushed into the chapel 'vi et armis' (with force and arms). They were overcome by the congregation, and some were kept prisoners in the chapel for the whole of the next day. Nineteen of them were charged with causing a riot, and appeared at the next Assizes, but what happened to them is not recorded. In the list of names of the rioters appears 'John le Clerk of Broghton, Magister, the Schoolmaster of Preston'. The reason for the riot is not known. Perhaps the rioters were friends of the murdered man, but here is certain evidence that there was a schoolmaster in Preston in 1358. It is interesting to note that he was a clerk of 'Broghton', which means that he was probably curate of Broughton Church, which was a Chapel of Ease for Preston Parish Church. Some later Masters were curates of other Chapels of Ease in the Parish.

The next Master of whom we have knowledge was Richard Marshall, or le Marishall who appears in the Guild Roll of 1397 as being admitted as a foreign burgess. He was described as 'clerk', but he must have been in minor Orders, as his two sons, John and Thomas are listed along with him in the Guild Roll of 1415. He was appointed Master of the School on 5 January 1400 (1399 in those days, since the year began on 25 March, and not on 1 January). The deed of appointment reads 'ad scolas gramaticales de Preston regendas'. The appointment was to be at the pleasure of the Archdeacon of Richmond, who had episcopal powers, and was the ecclesiastical authority for Preston at that time. Marshall was still Schoolmaster when he appeared in the Guild Roll of 1415. John le Marishall was Mayor in 1400, and was possibly a relation.

The only other Master that we know of in the fifteenth century was Thomas Preston. He received Letters Dimissory for Orders from Archbishop Neville of York in 1474. Letters Dimissory were issued by an Archbishop, or Bishop, authorising the bearer as a candidate for ordination.

Chapter 2

The Hoghton Chantry

IN MEDIEVAL TIMES it was the custom for pious persons to establish Chantries, by leaving money or land to provide a chapel in a church at which a priest would say mass regularly and pray for the souls of the founder and his family.

In 1450 a woman named Helen Masson entered into a clandestine marriage with Henry Hoghton esquire of Hoghton, at Preston Parish Church. The marriage was considered invalid because the consent of the father of the bridegroom had not been obtained, and Helen was therefore classed as a concubine. Henry succeeded his father in 1467, and in March 1468 he obtained a Papal Bull legitimizing the six children of the marriage.

Under Canon Law, where a couple were not validly married and had a child, a subsequent marriage between them would legitimize the child, provided that both the parents were free to marry at the time of the child's birth. This was known as legitimation 'per subsequens matrimonium', but there was no similar rule in the Common Law of England. At the Parliament held at Marlborough in 1267 the bishops proposed that a provision should be included in the statute to bring the Common Law into line with Canon Law in this respect, to which the barons replied 'Nolumus Leges Angliae mutare' (we will not alter the Laws of England), and the law was not altered until the Legitimacy Act of 1925. A Papal Bull was therefore necessary to establish legitimacy, and the obtaining of it indicates that the family must have been wealthy.

Henry died in 1479 aged about 52. Helen was alive at that time, but the date of her death is not known. However, she established a Chantry at the altar of the Blessed Virgin Mary in Preston Parish Church, where a priest was to celebrate continually for her soul, and for all Christian souls, and the incumbent was to be sufficiently learned in grammar to the intent to have a free grammar school kept there also. Presumably this was to take place from the date of her death, and as this is not known, the date of the foundation is assumed to be 1479.

The Chantry Certificate of 1546 describes the Chantry 'at the altar of our Ladie in the paroch church of Preston' as being 'of the foundacion of Helene Houghton, ther to celebrate contynuallie for hir sowle and all christen sowles, and th'incumbent thereof to be sufficiently lerned in gramar to th'entent to have a fre gramar skole kept ther also, as by the seyd foundacion it doth appere'. The value of the Chantry in the *Valor Ecclesiasticus* of 1535 was said to be £3 1s. per annum, and in 1548 it was £3 2s. 4d. It should be noted that the name of the foundress varies – she is called Helen Hoghton, Helene Houghton, and Helena de Hoghton in various documents. Norman Hodgson, when Headmaster (1926–1947) sometimes referred to her as 'The Blessed Helena Hoghton', but with what justification I cannot say. At some time after her death the Chantry passed into the possession of the Earls of Derby.

A priest named George Hale served at the Chantry from an unknown date until 1518 when he died, and he was then succeeded by Roger Levens or Lewyns. In 1528 Lewyns submitted a Statement of Complaint to the Chancellor of the Duchy in which he stated that Thomas, Earl of Derby, lately deceased, of his goodness, at the feast of St Luke the Evangelist, 1518, granted the Chantry of Our Lady within the Parish Church of Preston, belonging to his inheritances, with all rights and profits thereof, unto Lewyns, for doing Divine service duly in the said Chantry, all of which rights and profits he had had and occupied without let or trouble to any man. But of late, James Walton, Mayor of Preston, and others, Burgesses of Preston, along with divers riotous persons, to the number of 20 or more, with force and arms, to wit 'With billys and clubbs, swords, buklers, and oder defensible weapons' came on 2nd day of October last (i.e. 1527) to the Church of Preston, where Lewyns was 'in the end of his masse, and ther, before he couthe have space to do of his albe and amyce, violently broke one Cofur standing at his altur ende and entreed the same and wrongfully by might and great power, spoyled, toke, robbyd, and carried away with them from thense oon Chales of Sylver, and diverse vestments, masse bookes, and other juellez belongging to the said Chantry, and the keyes of the same. And if he had at that time made any resistaunce to their wrongful mysdemenor rehearsed and evill purpose prepensed, he had been by the said James Walton and the oders the said riotous persons put in danger and great perell of his lyve and to have been cruelly slain and murdered'. He also complained that James Walton had commanded the tenants of the Chantry lands not to pay their rents to him to his utter undoing. He therefore prayed for a writ of subpoena against the persons complained of.

James Walton, the Mayor, on his own behalf, and on behalf of the others concerned denied that he had ever heard of any such grant from the late Earl of Derby, and said that if any such were made 'it was null and void by reason that the town of Preston is an ancient borough corporate by the name of Mayor and Burgesses, time out of mind', which Mayor and Burgesses and other persons to their use were seized of certain lands and tenements in Preston and Walton to the yearly value of £6 in demesne as of fee, which they had of divers well disposed persons. In consideration whereof about 80 years ago (1448) the then Mayor and Burgesses 'of their charitable mind which they bore for the souls of those who had departed to God', agreed with the profits of the said lands to have a priest continually to sing and pray for the Mayor and Burgesses, and other inhabitants of the town, within the Church of Preston, and every priest appointed should keep a free school within the said town to teach the scholars there. After acknowledging the diligence wherewith the said priests had done their duty in this regard, the Mayor went on to state that of late, after the death of George Hale, clerk, the same service was void, and there was no priest there. By reason thereof the then Mayor and Burgesses 'were content at the instance of the said late Earl, to whom they were much bounden, to accept such a priest as he would appoint'.

Accordingly the Earl appointed Roger Lewyns, the plaintiff, who would not keep the free school, and do other divine service as former priests had done. Such being the case, the Mayor, at the time mentioned, after the said Sir Roger had fully ended his mass and was 'avoided and gone' from the altar 'in peasable manner, thinking no evil to no person, toke the said chales, as it was wrapped and inclosid on the altar,' and delivered it to Richard Fedeler, one of the wardens of the said Church, 'among other the chales, vestments, and ornaments to the said Church belonging'. After the delivery of the chalice Lewyns had used it again, and had put it, and the vestments, in a chest appointed for the priest. The Mayor admitted that he had bade the tenants and farmers of the chantry lands not to pay their rents to Lewyns, and considered that it was lawful for him so to do, for the reasons given. He concluded by plainly denying that the Earl of Derby had a perpetual Chantry in Preston Church.

In his counter-reply Lewyns again asserted that the Earl of Derby, not only in his own right, but also with the consent of the Mayor and Burgesses of Preston, gave him the said Chantry for life, and he had enjoyed the rights and profits of the same, peaceably for three years and more.

The result of the Chancery action is not known. It seems clear that the Hoghton Chantry had become the property of the Earl of Derby, and that he had appointed Lewyns with the approval of the Corporation. The denial of the existence of the Hoghton Chantry is therefore untrue. The Chantry that the Mayor claimed had been founded by the Corporation in about 1448 is not mentioned elsewhere, and certainly was not noted by the Commissioners, who were very thorough. It may have been a figment of the Mayor's imagination, but that is not to say that the Corporation was not providing £6 per annum for the schoolmaster, since the Corporation had been paying for a school since long before the establishment of the Hoghton Chantry, and the £3 or so per annum provided by the Chantry funds was hardly enough to pay a priest cum schoolmaster.

It is also clear that Lewyns was not performing his duty of running the school – a fact that he does not deny in his counter statement. The action of the Mayor, and those with him must, therefore, have arisen out of considerable exasperation.

The date of this occurrence is given as 1522 in the Chetham Society volume OS 60, and in Smith's 'Records'. The earl died in that year, and Lewyns was appointed parish chaplain or curate, of Slaidburn in 1523/4 and might, therefore, have left Preston then, but 1527 is the most likely date since that was the year when James Walton was Mayor, and is the date given in the Victoria County History.

In the *Valor Ecclesiasticus* of 1535 Nicholas Banestre was stated to be 'cantorist' and schoolmaster. He was born in 1506, and probably came from the family that had provided some 11 Mayors of Preston since 1346.

In 1548 the Chantry possessed no plate (one wonders where the 'Chales of Syluer' had gone), and the lands held were as follows:

Thomas Comball, one burgage lying in Preston	10s.	
Richard Powle, 3 acres of land there	5s.	
Ralph Comball, one burgage there	6s.	8d.
John Harrison, one cottage there	3s.	4d.
Robert Chadwick, one burgage there	5s.	
William Slater, one acre of land there	3s.	
Roger Mason, 2 roods there	1s.	4d.
George Salter, one acre of land there	1s.	6d.
John Johnson, 2 roods of land there	1s.	
Henry Preston, one rood there		8d.
Richard Thornborough, 2 roods of ground there	1s.	
Richard Melling, one acre of ground lying in the Ley	5s.	
Thomas Alcock, 3 acres of ground lying in Fishwick	4s.	
Henry Bank, one tenement, with appurtenances, lying in Walton, near Preston	14s.	10d.

An Act was passed in 1545 to abolish all Chantries, with the intention that the Crown would seize the properties that supported them. This Act was not implemented, but it was replaced by the Chantries Act of 1548 which confiscated all the Chantry lands, with some exceptions in favour of certain colleges and cathedrals. This had an unfortunate effect because many of the Chantries, as in Preston, provided education, and, although promises were made, very little was done by the government to provide new schools. In Preston the lands of the Chantry were leased to William Kenyon for 21 years from Easter 1549, but by a warrant signed by Sir Walter Mildmay and Robert Kelway on 11 August 1548 and addressed to the Chancellor of the Duchy it was stated 'that a Grammar Scole hath heretofore been continually kept in the parish of Preston with the revenues of the chauntry of Our Lady founded in the church there and that the Scolemaster there had for his wages yerely of the revenues of the same chauntry £2 16s. 2 ¼d. which scole is very meete and necessary to continue'. It was therefore ordered that 'the same scole shall continue and that Nicholas Banister, Scolemaster there, shall be and remayne in the same rowme and that he shall have for his stipend and wages 56s. 2d. yearly'. This was duly paid from the Duchy accounts until 1558. It is clear from this that there was no gap between the cessation of the Chantry, and the continuation of the School under the new arrangements.

In 1553, when Mary I came to the throne, the Mayor, Lawrence Banastre (possibly the schoolmaster's brother) and the Corporation applied to the Duchy Court to have the lease of the Chantry lands set aside on the ground that for the last 100 years there had been a free school in Preston 'for the educacion and bryngyng up of young children' with lands worth 5 marks (£3 6s. 8d.) per year, and that William Kenyon had 'by sinister means' proved that these lands were part of the Chantry endowment, and had obtained his lease 'to the great injury of the inhabitants and bringing up of yong children of the towne and the countrye nyghe adjoyning'. The application failed because it was clear that the lands did form part of the Chantry endowment. In 1558 the Chantry lands were granted to the Savoy Hospital.

It appears from the statements of the Mayor in 1528, and the Mayor in 1553 that there may have been two endowments connected with the school, namely one provided by the Corporation about 1448, and the one provided by Helen Hoghton about 1479, and that these two had become mixed in the minds of the members of the Corporation. This would account for the mention of £6 in 1528, whereas the Hoghton grant was only worth £3 2s. 4d.

As mentioned above the payment to Nicholas Banastre ceased in 1558. The amount is entered in the accounts of the Duchy for the next two years, but is struck out as not paid. The reason for this appears to be the change in religion that occurred when Elizabeth I came to the throne in 1558. Strype in his *Annals* (1567) states 'In Lancashire papists about here numerous. Mass commonly said. Priests harboured'. In 1561 Banastre had been found to be a 'recusant at large', an 'Unlerned scolemaster', and a rank Jesuit. He was confined to the County of Lancaster, the town of Preston excepted, and must therefore have been deprived of his office of schoolmaster. In 1567/68 the Bishop of Chester held a visitation to see that 'no obstinate persons having been justly deprived of offices of ministry be secretly maintained', and the name of Banastre appears among those priests who had been refused the ministry because of 'the contempt and evil opinion' which they had of religion.

Chapter 3

Elizabeth I to the Restoration

I N THE GUILD ROLL of 1562 the Schoolmaster is named as William Clayton, who must have succeeded Nicholas Banastre at some time between 1558 and 1562. He was admitted as an inhabitant burgess, so he was probably not a native Prestonian. He does not appear in the Guild Roll of 1582.

Clayton was succeeded by Peter Carter, M. A., who came to Preston from Wigan in 1587, and continued in office until his death in September 1590. He was born in Lancashire about 1530, and attended St John's College, Cambridge where he took his degrees, and in 1554 was elected Assheton Fellow. In 1573 he published a book consisting of annotations on the dialectic of John Seton. This John Seton (1498–1567) was also a fellow of St John's College where he taught philosophy. He was a devout Catholic, and was chaplain to Gardiner, Bishop of Winchester. In 1554 he was sent to Oxford to hold disputations with Cranmer, Latimer, and Ridley before their martyrdoms. After the accession of Elizabeth I he was imprisoned, but escaped to Rome. Carter's book was dedicated to the Earl of Derby, and was no doubt a criticism of Seton's beliefs, since to hold office as Schoolmaster Carter must have been a supporter of the new religious settlement. He was buried in the churchyard of the Parish Church, and Dodsworth records that the following inscription was 'engraven on a fair stone supported with four corner stones, half-a-yard fro the ground in ye church yard':

> Hoc monumentum tegit P. C. Cantabrigien'
> Magestrum in artibus Socium Colleg' S. Jo
> annotationu' in Io Sct: Logic. Authore'
> Prestonie ludimag' mortuu' juxta annu'
> Aetatis LX anno dom'i 1590, Sepult' octo. Sept.

(This memorial covers Peter Carter Master of Arts of Cambridge, Fellow of St John's College, author of annotations to John Seton's Logic. Schoolmaster of Preston. Died near to his sixtieth birthday in the year of our Lord 1590, and buried on 8 September.)

The successor of Peter Carter was William Gellibrand (or Gelibrand) who came from Ramsgreave near Blackburn. He had been at Brasenose College, Oxford, and became a Bachelor of Arts there on 14 January 1569. He is listed as Schoolmaster on the Guild Roll of 1602. He was described as a 'stallenger' or stranger, and had to pay sevenpence to be enrolled. On 26 August 1607, he was appointed Rector of Warrington and left Preston, although his two sons seem to have remained, because they are both entered on the Guild Roll of 1622.

Henry Yates succeeded Gellibrand in 1607, but little is known of him. He died in 1616, and was buried on 6 July. It was during his time that new arrangements were made by the Borough Council for the payment of the Schoolmaster. The Mayor was assisted by two Bailiffs, appointed each year, and by ancient custom the Bailiffs were required to provide, at their own expense, 'wine beer, cheese, bread, and ale' every Easter, not only for the Mayor and Burgesses, but also for strangers. In August 1612 it was decided to alter this duty, which was, no doubt, proving expensive. The decision is set out in the White Book of the Corporation as follows:

26 Aug 1612. Whereas heretofore of ancient time it hath been used and accustomed within the town of Preston, that the Bailiffs thereof, for the time being, at the feast of Easter, yearly should, to their great and excessive charge, provide wine, beer, bread, cheese, ale and other Banquetting stuff and provision, as well for the Mayor and his brethren the Common Council and all other the free Burgesses, as also for all strangers, passengers, and neighbours repairing to the same town, by reason whereof the concourse and assembly of people at the same time, did grow great, very turbulent and unruly tending not only to the break of His Majesty's peace but also divers other inconvenience thereof very likely to ensue to the great prejudice of the whole Corporation, and the peaceable government thereof: for the avoidance thereof, and to the end that the now Bailiffs of this town and all others which hereafter shall be Bailiffs may be eased of that great and unnecessary charge by them heretofore disbursed, and that some smaller and lesser sum of money may be yearly, for ever, given and paid by the same Bailiffs and their successors, and to a more godly laudable and charitable purpose. It is therefore ordered by Henry Breres gent., now Mayor of the said town and his Brethren the Common Council, that William Lemon and Henry Ingham now Bailiffs, in consideration that they have been eased of that unnecessary charge of the said banquet at Easter last, that the said William Lemon and Henry Ingham shall immediately pay to the now Schoolmaster of this town the sum of Twenty Marks [a mark was one-third of a pound, i.e. 6s. 8d.], in part payment of his stipend and wages, that is to say either of them £6 13s. 4d. and that all persons which hereafter shall be Bailiffs, shall from henceforth be eased of the said banquet at Easter, and in consideration thereof shall pay to the Schoolmaster at the feast of Easter yearly £13 6s. 8d., i.e. either of the Bailiffs £6 13s. 4d. If any future Bailiff refuse to pay the same to the Schoolmaster, then the said Bailiff or Bailiffs shall keep the said banqueting in the Hall belonging to the said town for the Mayor, his

Common Council, and the Burgesses inhabitants and such other gentlemen and others of account, as may be invited by the said Mayor or any of the Common Council at the same time of Easter.

It seems from the latter part of this Order that, although the banquets open to all comers were to cease, the Bailiffs had the alternative of providing a banquet to the select few instead of paying the money to the Schoolmaster. Some difficulties may have arisen as a result of this decision because it was repeated at the Guild of 1642.

These provisions seem clear enough, but only eight years later they were challenged by William Curtis, who was one of the Bailiffs for the year 1650. He publicly refused to pay his portion of the Schoolmaster's salary, and was informed by the Council that if he persisted in his contumacy a forced sale of his goods and chattels would be made to meet the claim, and the costs incurred in securing the money. The amount specified was £10. An Act had been passed in 1649 to improve the salaries of Schoolmasters, and it may be that this inspired Curtis to make his stand. However on 16 July 1652 the Council revoked the previous Order which was 'conceyved to bee dissonant to ye Lawes of this Nacon'. It was ordered:

That the sum of £22 of current English money shalbee paid unto the said Schoolemaster yearely . . . out of ye Revenues of this Towne by the Baylives thereof, yearely for the tyme being, in lieu of theis somes following, formerly payable by them forth of the Revenues of this Towne, vizt. £6 13s. 4d. formerly payable to the Schoolemaster, £5 6s. 8d. usually payable to ye Baylives for their yearely fees and weekly wages and 40s. yearely payable to the steward of this Towne, and £6 yearely payable to ye Usher of the said Schoole; and also the said Steward haveing the benefitt of the Corts and other profitts formerly accustomed to ye said Steward (excepting th'formenconed some of 40s.) is to allow and pay to the said Schoolemaster yearely if his availes [i.e. profits of the courts], will amount to soe much, the some of 40s.

It is clear from the above that by this time there was an Usher or Assistant Master at the School. Shortly afterwards the Schoolmaster's stipend was raised to £30.

To return to the Masters – Hugh Whalley was described as Schoolmaster in the Guild Roll of 1622, and presumably had succeeded Henry Yates on the latter's death in 1616. It was at this period that James I came to Preston during his visit to Lancashire. (This was the occasion when he is alleged to have knighted the loin of beef at Hoghton Tower.) On 15 August 1617 he was received at the Market Cross and heard a speech by Mr Breres the Recorder. He was then presented with 'a Bowll', and attended a banquet in the Guild Hall. It is said (but I can find no authority for this) that the

King saw the boys of the Grammar School, and said that the senior boys
'lackit dignity', and he therefore decreed that in future they should wear
gowns. It is quite possible that the boys were included in the parade which
welcomed the King, and this may indeed be the origin of the blue gowns
worn by the prefects of the School, although I recall that Norman Hodgson
(Headmaster 1926–1947) used to say that there was a picture somewhere of
a senior boy wearing a green gown. (See Chapter 14 for further reference
to gowns.)

Hugh Whalley is described as 'gentleman', so he was probably not in holy
orders. As mentioned above he appears in the Guild Roll for 1622 as
Schoolmaster, with his two sons. The next name in the Roll is William
Walker who is described as 'Hipodidasculus' which Fishwick translates as
'horse trainer'. However in the Victoria County History the name is given
as William Walton, and the Latin description is translated not as 'horse trainer',
but rather as 'boy trainer', in other words an Usher or Assistant Master.
The accuracy of this is confirmed by the fact that an usher certainly existed
in 1652.

Hugh Whalley was appointed to the Headmastership of Kirkham Grammar
School in 1636, but he was strongly opposed by Edward Fleetwood, the
Vicar of Kirkham, who tried to keep him out of office by locking the door
of the school, and by writing to the Bishop accusing Whalley of being
tainted with popery, and therefore likely to corrupt the children rather than
educate them. The Bishop found that Whalley was a communicating member
of the Church of England, and confirmed his appointment.

He was succeeded by Roger Sherburne, who appears in the Guild Roll
of 1642. Nothing is known of him, and he probably left in 1649, because
in 1650 the Schoolmaster to whom William Curtis refused to pay his
proportion of the stipend was William Robinson.

By 1656 the Schoolmaster was named Winckley. This is known because
the register of St John's College, Cambridge contains an entry relating to
the admission of Elisha Clarkson, son of John Clarkson, draper of Preston.
Clarkson was fifteen at the time of his entry on 23 April 1661, and is said
to have been taught by Winckley for six years.

Chapter 4

1660–1704

SINCE THE ABOLITION of the Hoghton Chantry in 1548 the School does not appear to have had any income other than that provided by the Corporation. This state of affairs was changed when Bartholomew Worthington, a shoemaker by trade, by a codicil to his will made in 1663, having instructed his wife to build an almshouse, gave to her, for life, a close of land in Broadgate, said to contain one and a half acres, which he held on a 99-year lease. Upon her death the income was to be devoted to the augmentation of the wages of the Master and Masters of the Free Grammar School, and he desired the Mayor and Aldermen to see that this was carried into effect.

Worthington must have been a man of some wealth because he was one of the principal lenders of money to a fund raised in 1635 for meeting the cost of a renewal of the Town's Charter (which never took place). He was a member of the Council, and his arms are included in a stained glass window in the Parish Church. He held land on Fishergate Hill, and in January 1654, and again in November 1656 he was ordered by the Court Leet 'to remove his midden in front of his barn there'. In 1654 he was also ordered to prevent his 'copp' in the weind leading to 'Minspit well' (presumably Main Sprit Weind) sliding into the highway. In the 28th year of Charles II (1676–77) the Corporation purchased the freehold of the land bequeathed by Worthington, from John Cottam, and it was let for £12 or £14 per year.

The land was known as the School Fields, and, although it was said to be in Broadgate, it clearly was not in the modern road called Broadgate which runs along the bank of the Ribble. It is shown on a map of 1774 as being on the southern side of what is now Fishergate, with a very narrow frontage to the street. It was just to the west of the Bar (or gate) which was where Fishergate terminated at that time, the continuation beyond the Bar being called Fishergate Lane.

It is as well to complete the history of the land here. On 4 July 1800 the Council appointed a Committee to examine the fields at Fishergate Bars belonging to the School, in relation to an application made by Messrs. Wren and Corry. The Committee reported on 11 September, but the matter was reserved for further consideration. On 2 July 1801 another Committee was appointed to consider a proposal by the same two men respecting a wall

and tunnel proposed to be built over the ditch at the School House. On
11 September 1801 the Council agreed to lease the land to Wren and Corry
'for ever' at a rent of 3d. per square yard (if the land did consist of one and
a half acres this would yield £90 15s. 0d. per annum). However on 4
October 1802 the Council agreed to lease part of the land to the Lancaster
Canal Company for £180. On 15 April 1803 the Council decided to sue
Wren and Corry for cutting turf on the Town Moor, but the action was
settled on payment of £20 by the defendants (which was paid back to them
in 1809). On 22 January 1808 Wren and Corry let part of the School Field
to Mrs Mary Hall, who was to pay a rent of £1 10s. 0d. to the Corporation,
and on 19 February 1808 they let another part to Robert Salter who was
to pay £1 11s. 0d. to the Corporation. In 1805 the Corporation sold 'part
of a close formerly called Johnson's Hey, but then known as the School
Field on the south side of Broad Gate Lane' to John Addison and William
St Clare for the purpose of erecting a playhouse thereon (this would be the
Theatre Royal). The plot sold consisted of 800 square yards, and was to be
subject to a yearly rental of £10. Fishwick states that the other parts of the
School land were in the same year sold, and made to realize an income of
£55 1s. 6d. per year which, according to the Charity Commissioners' Report
in 1823, was paid to the Headmaster. This is confirmed by Baines in 1825
who says 'On this land the theatre and the houses adjoining southwards
have since been built, and the property now yields a rent of £55 1s. 6d.
yearly, exclusive of the sum of £180 paid to the Corporation by the Lancaster
Canal Company for a small part of the field, and for which capital sum the
Corporation pay £9 a year interest to the Headmaster of the Grammar
School'. Whittle in 1837 states 'They [the Corporation] are also possessed
of the following charitable funds – freehold property consisting of fields
termed the "School Fields" bequeathed for the support of a Free Grammar
School: these produce annually £46 3s. 0d., which amount is included in
the Corporation rental: the proceeds are paid to the head master, together
with a voluntary annual donation from the Corporation of £45. A house
was bequeathed for the same purpose, and the master of the school is allowed
to occupy this rent free. The estimated value of which house annually is
£30' In 1857 Hardwick states that the 1855 accounts of the Corporation
also show the income to be £46 3s. 0d. plus £9 from the land sold to the
Canal Company. This is a most complicated story, and raises a number of
questions, since the Corporation seem to have leased or sold the land to a
number of people. The tangle is now too difficult to unravel.

It is not known where the school was originally situated, but it was
probably held in the Parish Church in the early days. Later according to
S. Sartin in *Historic Preston*. it was in a building in Crooked Lane.

In 1666 the Corporation built a new school building on waste land at the bottom of Stonygate, near to the churchyard. The site is also stated to be in Syke Hill (which is at the bottom of Stonygate), and opposite Kendall Well. The Syke was a stream called Avenham Syke which ran at the bottom of Stonygate, and joined the Ribble at the bottom of Fishergate Hill. Dr Kuerden in his description of Preston in the 1680s states 'This burrough is likewise adorned with a spacious wel built or rather re-edifyed church, for the decent and more comodious solemnization of religious rytes and instruction of the people in sound and healthful Christian doctrines, and nereunto this church there is likewise built a large and hansom schoole house, for the better education of their children, and bringing them up in humane learning, making them fitter for trade or other better preferment in the world'. The school apparently had two schoolrooms, one above and one below.

There must have been two earlier School buildings for it is recorded that in 1650 James Hodgkinson was the Corporation's tenant of 'the old schole house and two bays of buildings adjoining to it' (this may be the building in Crooked Lane). Furthermore the Court Leet, at a sitting on 4 May 1655 decided – 'The Bailiffs shall see the cawsall repaired on Stonygate to the milne field gate, and to the schoole before the 24 June next, else to pay 6s. 8d.'

William Yates was possibly the Headmaster when the new school was built as he is described as 'pedagogus' in the Guild Roll of 1662. He was followed by Richard Taylor, who was replaced by William Barrowe in 1675. The latter was only 22 at the time, having obtained his BA degree in 1673 at Corpus Christi College, Oxford. He resigned in 1677, and was replaced by George Walmesley on 10 May. Walmesley had attended Jesus College, Cambridge, as a sizar, and became Bachelor of Arts in 1675. In 1679 he became Master of Arts, and decided to take Holy Orders. Apparently the Corporation did not wish to have as Headmaster a clergyman who was also holding an ecclesiastical office, and on 17 November 1680 he was told that he must resign by 7 February 1681. He chose to resign at once, and his successor was elected on 6 December 1680. This was Richard Croston (or Croxton) who had taken his BA degree at Emmanuel College, Cambridge in 1674. His salary was fixed at £30 per year, plus the income from the Worthington land. He took orders a year later, but, unlike Walmesley, he was not required to resign, and was permitted to preach sermons with the consent of the Mayor. He continued in office until 1689. In that year he refused to swear allegiance to William and Mary, and thus became a non-juror, and was accordingly dismissed.

In Kuerden's description of the Guild of 1682 is the first mention of the participation of the boys of the School in the ceremonies. On the first day of the Guild the Mayor Aldermen and Councillors marched in formal procession from the Town Hall to Churchgate Bar where a scholar of the Grammar School made a speech, and a hogshead of 'nappy ale' (strong or foaming ale) was broached, of which the Mayor drank a glass. The procession then marched to Fishergate Bar where another speech was made by a scholar, and more ale was drunk. The same procedure was followed at Friargate Bar, and the procession then returned to the Market Cross where a barrel of wine was broached, and the Headmaster gave a 'learned speech and verses concerning the prosperous Government of his Majesty (Charles II) and his gracious confirmation of their unparalleled franchises of a Guild Merchant'. It was perhaps from this occasion that the custom arose of the Head Boy of the School making a Latin oration during the Guild celebrations, which continued until the Guild of 1952.

Thomas Whitehead, BA of Jesus College Cambridge was appointed Headmaster on 30 September 1689, but Thomas Lodge was appointed on 4 November in the same year, so that Whitehead either never took up office, or left after a few weeks. Lodge had been Headmaster of Lancaster Grammar School, and remained at Preston until he resigned in 1698.

Norman Hodgson used to say that one of his predecessors had been accused of murder, but that what had happened to him was not known. The original of this story was Edward Denham, a Londoner, who was a King's Scholar at Eton, and a fellow of King's College Cambridge (BA 1693, MA 1697). He was appointed Headmaster on 19 September 1698, and resigned when he was elected to be Headmaster of Macclesfield Grammar School on 6 July 1704. In the Minute Book of the Governors of Macclesfield Grammar School it is recorded, on 11 December 1712, that Denham had been charged with the wilful murder of Thomas Davye, and was then in prison, so that he was incapacitated from fulfilling his office. An assistant was therefore appointed to take his place during his incapacity. In fact he died in prison at Chester Castle on 22 April 1717. He could not have been found guilty of murder, because that would have meant that he would have been hanged, since murder was not then an offence for which he could have 'pleaded his clergy'. It is likely then that he was convicted, not of murder, but of manslaughter, for which he was imprisoned – one wonders if he killed one of his schoolboys.

During this period the Corporation had taken further interest in the improvement of the School. In July 1690 a new building, 24 feet by 18 feet was erected adjoining the schoolhouse, which, with the attached garden, was to be used by the Headmaster. Kuerden describes this as follows: 'there has been annexed to it (the schoolhouse) an handsome fabric adjoining to it, as a fitting habitation for a schoolmaster, for convenience and ease over the school, a fitting place for the scholars' retirement, for making their exercises, as likewise upon occasion if needful for a scrivener to make use of with least prejudice to the scholars as to their absence or attendance'. A scrivener was a professional penman, but could also be a legal stationer, or one who arranged mortgages. The question therefore arises as to whether the scrivener in this case was one who taught penmanship to the boys, or one who carried out his occupation in part of the building when it was not required by the School. By some historians (in particular Berry) this building has been confused with the house for the Headmaster which was built in 1728, and which is referred to later. This is clearly an error because Francis Gastrell, who was appointed Bishop of Chester in 1714, prepared a list of all churches and schools etc. in his diocese, and with regard to the School states 'Free school taught by Master and Usher nominated by Council. Master £30 more or less at discretion of Mayor and Council plus house, and field worth £6 given by Worthington in 1663 – Usher £13 6s. 8d.' As Gastrell died in 1725 this reference must be to the earlier house added to the School in 1690.

In 1698 the Council passed a most important resolution:

ORDERS TO BE OBSERVED IN PRESTON SCHOOL
Agreed at a meeting of the Mayor and Council the 19th day of September 1698. By the Mayor, Aldermen and Common Council whose names are subscribed viz:

1. That every scholar fail not in coming to School from Lady Day to Michaelmas at half an hour past six, and from Michaelmas to Lady Day at half an hour past seven of the clock in the morning, and there continue till eleven, or longer if the business of the School require.

2. That they come again at one every afternoon and stay till five at night winter and summer, unless it be on such afternoons the following orders do except.

3. That on Thursday in the afternoon they continue at School no longer than three of the clock, and on Saturday in the afternoon not come at all, unless upon any omission of their duty they deserve confinement or be then ordered to perform some school exercise there.

4. That the whole time they are in School they behave themselves decently, neither playing, prating with one another, or getting their lessons with such a loud voice as to disturb others.

5. That both in and out of School they avoid gaming, fighting, swearing, lying and all profane, obscene and scurrilous expressions.

6. That they all come to church on Sundays, all church holydays, breaking up, and other play days which are granted, and there decently behave themselves.

7. That no one boy absent himself from School at any time, or on any account without leave first asked by his parents or friends.

8. That leave to play be not granted above one day in a week, nor that if a church holyday fall in that week, and that whoever (except the Mayor, Bailiffs, and scholars going to the University) obtains a play, do give two shillings and sixpence to be laid out in books for the use of the School.

9. That the weekly monitor have a roll of the scholars' names, that it be called over every morning and afternoon in School, and the names of those that are absent set down in a scroll of paper, likewise of those that are absent from church, come too late, behave themselves insolently, resort to ale-houses, play at football or cast stones in the church-yard, or otherwise misconduct themselves.

10. That the scholars be catechized every week, according to the Church Catechism, in English, Greek, or Latin according to their capacities.

11. That none cut break or deface any seat, desk, ceiling, door, floor, wall, windows etc. of the School House, or any buildings belonging to it.

12. That barring out for Christmas (which has heretofore occasioned much misbehaviour and mischief) be forbidden, and such scholars as shall hereafter attempt any thing of that nature to be severely chastised, and in case of obstinacy to be absolutely expelled the School. And for the future these vacations be observed (to wit), Monday before Christmas Day and till the day after the Twelfth Day, unless that day fall to be on the Saturday or Sunday, and in such case the School to open on the Monday next after. At Shrovetide in all five days. At Easter five days in the whole. At Whitsuntide three weeks in the whole. Three days at Summer Fayre, and two days at Winter Fayre.

13. That at the long vacation at Whitsuntide the boys learn to write, that this being fixed on as the most convenient for a writing master to teach the boys of this School.

14. That all scholars throughout the whole School do show a perfect submission to the Headmaster, as well in matters that relate to learning as governing them, and that the scholars under the Middle Master, and the Usher or Lower Master, do submit to their several Masters both as to teaching, and to correction while they are under their discipline, but the Headmaster to have the superintendence and government, and if he be absent then the rule thereof to fall to the Middle Master.

15. And to the end the discipline of the place may better be maintained, and ill example to others be avoided, it is ordered that whoever rebels against, and openly resists the Master shall (for the public good of the

School) be immediately expelled, and not readmitted but on a submission that shall satisfy the Master.

16. And that these Orders be fixed openly in the School and read openly to the scholars twice a year (viz) before breaking up at Whitsuntide and Christmas, and if any of the scholars or any other by their consent or encouragement shall tear, pull down, obliterate, or otherwise deface these Orders such scholars to be expelled, and any other person offending to be punished by the Mayor.

17. That the several Masters of the School do observe such Rules and Orders as the Mayor, Aldermen and Common Council shall from time to time think fit to make touching the discipline and government of the said School.

Signed by the Mayor, Aldermen and Common Councillors.

'Barring-out' is described by Dr Johnson in his life of Addison as follows: 'The practice of barring-out was a savage licence, practised in many schools to the end of the last century (i.e. the seventeenth century) by which the boys, when the periodical vacation drew near, growing petulant at the approach of liberty, some days before the time of regular recess, took possession of the school, of which they barred the doors, and bade their master defiance from the windows. It is not easy to suppose that on such occasions the master would do more than laugh; yet if tradition may be credited, he often struggled hard to force or surprise the garrison'. Addison planned and conducted a barring-out at Lichfield School about 1685. The custom continued and a barring-out took place at Preston in the 1780s (see Chapter 17 – Edward Baines). Something similar must have happened at Greyfriars in more modern times as there is a book entitled *Billy Bunter's Barring-out*. 'Sit-ins' by University students are, no doubt, the modern equivalent.

Chapter 5

1704–1778

THE NEXT HEADMASTER was William Powell who succeeded Denham in 1704, and of whom little is known. He was followed by Edward Mainwaring of Whitmore in Staffordshire who had been admitted as a Fellow Commoner to St John's College, Cambridge at the age of seventeen on 17 July 1699. It is not known whether or not he took a degree, but he was elected Headmaster on 30 August 1708 at the age of twenty-four, at a salary of £30 per annum, plus the house, and £6 in respect of the Worthington bequest. On 23 August 1716 his salary was reduced to £20 per annum because of his misbehaviour, but what this constituted is not known. On 4 November 1719 the Council relented, and put his salary back to £30. On 10 September 1724 he petitioned the Council, pointing out the fact that his salary had been reduced for three years and that of late he had applied himself with diligence to advance the credit and reputation of the School, and asking that he might have the money, that had been deducted, paid to him. The Council agreed to this, but he only remained in office until 1726, when he left to become Headmaster of Birmingham School.

To replace Mainwaring the Council called on the services of Daniel Pulteney, one of the Members of Parliament for Preston. Through his acquaintances at Oxford he obtained recommendations from Dr Tenry and Dr Gregory, the Professor of Modern History, who suggested William Davies from St Asaph, who had attended Westminster School, and had entered Christ Church College, Oxford on 30 June 1708 at the age of seventeen. He graduated BA in 1712, and MA in 1715. He was willing to accept the Headmastership provided that the salary was increased to £50. The Council agreed to this figure, inclusive of the rent of the land, on 12 September 1726. He was not happy with this, and on 11 November 1726 the Council agreed that he should have £50 plus the house, and the rent of the land. He resigned, after eleven years, in 1737, and moved to an ecclesiastical living in Herefordshire.

It was during his time at Preston that a new house for the Headmaster was built in Stonygate. This was paid for by a public subscription, to which the Corporation contributed £50. It was (or rather is, since it still stands), a substantial double fronted three storey building which provided, not only accommodation for the Headmaster and his family, but also room for boarders.

Robert Oliver was born in 1710, and entered Worcester College, Oxford on 15 June 1727, later going to Merton College, where he obtained his MA degree on 24 May 1734. On 20 June in the same year he became Vicar of Warton-in-Lonsdale (presumably the village just north of Carnforth). On 18 February 1737 he was appointed Headmaster by the Council. On 23 June 1744 he also became curate of St George's Church. This had been built in 1723 as a Chapel of Ease for the Parish Church. He thus held three appointments at the same time, and at St George's he was to read prayers daily, preach twice on Sundays (except on sacrament days when he had to assist at the Parish Church), and to read special prayers on holydays, and on Wednesdays and Fridays.

On Wednesday 11 June 1746 he preached a sermon at St. George's entitled 'Subject to the Government – a Duty', and this was published in book form – possibly the first book published in Preston. It must have had a political content in support of the Whig Government of the day, and was, therefore, contrary to the views of the Council which supported the Tories.

On 3 February 1747, after receiving a report on him, the Council resolved that he be removed from his place as Schoolmaster. The reason for this was said to be the the state and condition of the School, and that the conduct of the Masters was very grave. Oliver was said to be receiving £90 per annum from salary, rents, cock-pennies, and fees. (Cock-pennies were financial contributions made to schoolmasters by their pupils, so called because the money was supposed to be used to purchase fighting cocks.) The Second Master was Thomas Harrison, and it was found that out of the 67 boys in the School he was responsible for 50, and the Headmaster was responsible for only 17. Furthermore Oliver never took any interest in the boys that Harrison taught, although several of them were between 10 and 14 years of age. He had changed the School hours, as laid down in the Orders of 1698, and usually came into School at 8 or 9 a. m., and then went out to breakfast where he often stayed for up to an hour. He left at 11 a. m., and did not return until 2 p. m. He closed the School as soon as it was too dark to read by daylight, instead of keeping it open until 5.30 p. m. He allowed an excessive number of holidays, and it was calculated that schooldays had not exceeded half of the year. The report noted that Harrison, the Usher, was carrying out his work very satisfactorily, although only paid £13 6s. 8d., and cock-pennies. The report concluded by saying that the School was greatly decayed, and had lost its previous good reputation, so that many gentlemen and tradesmen sent their children out of town to other schools. As a result the Council ordered that Oliver should be dismissed from the 1 August 1747, but his salary was to be suspended from the date of the Order.

One unstated reason for the dismissal was undoubtedly political. His views must have been clear from the sermon mentioned above and at the

Parliamentary election in 1747, at which two Tory M. P's were elected, with the support of the Council, Oliver had canvassed for their Whig opponents. The Council no doubt felt that its employees should support the candidates that it supported.

Oliver refused to leave, and preached the Assize sermon at Lancaster on 21 March 1749, being described on the printed copy of the sermon as 'Headmaster of the Preston Grammar School'. He also appears to have been occupying the post in 1764, because on 7 February in that year he wrote a long letter to the Council in which he stated that the real difference between himself and the Council was that he had canvassed and voted for the Whig candidate at the 1747 Parliamentary election. In this letter he resigned as Headmaster, but there was a dispute as to the part of his salary which had not been paid, and he threatened legal action. On 7 August 1764 the Council decided to seek the advice of Counsel on the matter. It was resolved as follows: 'It is the sense of the Mayor and Council now present that the acceptance of the keys of the School, and School House from the Rev. Mr Oliver shall not be construed to an admission of his having held by right since the order of discharge, but on the contrary it is the sense of the Council that he has not been in any way entitled to any arrears since such discharge, and he has since that time kept illegal possession'.

It appears from this that Oliver had continued as Headmaster for seventeen years without pay, but had kept the house, and received fees from non-free scholars, and the cock-pennies.

When the new Headmaster was appointed in 1765 it is stated that the post had been vacant for some years. It cannot have been a happy time for the School. Oliver would not have suffered much financially because he was a confirmed pluralist. On 24 September 1765 he became Vicar of St Michael's-on-Wyre, and on 2 April 1768 transferred from there to become Rector of Whittington-in-Lonsdale, retaining Warton-in-Lonsdale, and St George's.

In June 1745 an advertisement for an Usher appeared in *Preston Journal or True British Courant* (published by Robert Moon) – 'An applicant to show himself well recommended as to his moral character, and that he has a competent knowledge of the classic authors'. This must have been an advertisement for a third master, because Thomas Harrison was replaced on 29 December 1750 by Thomas Fleetwood, and died in 1752.

The replacement for Oliver was Ellis Henry of Wrexham, who was born in 1743, and took his BA at Brasenose College, Oxford in 1763. He was appointed Headmaster on 10 June 1765. A reference was received from Mr Clayton of Manchester under whose care he had passed the whole of his scholastic education, and who said that his behaviour and proficiency in good learning thoroughly recommended him. Good references were also received from the Rev. Dr Yarborough, the Principal of Brasenose College, and others. He was appointed 'during the will and pleasure of the Mayor, Aldermen and Capital Burgesses, or the greater part thereof', and it was stated that it was lawful for him to be dismissed without reasons being stated. He was to have possession of the School building, except for the lower room which was let to Robert Shepherd, who was a writing, and accountancy teacher. Oddly enough the White Book shows that Henry was again appointed on the 6 and 26 September 1765, and still again on 19 May 1766. In the latter case he may have resigned, and then thought better of it. He finally resigned on 13 November 1770, and was replaced by Thomas Fleetwood the Second Master, who took office as Headmaster on 7 January 1771. His salary was only £45 per annum unlike the salary of £50 that had been paid to his predecessor, but then he does not seem to have had a degree.

In January 1768 Henry let some rooms in the Headmaster's house to Richard Arkwright. The latter was born in Lord Street, Preston on 23 September 1732. Starting life as a barber, he became a dealer in hair for the making of wigs, and left Preston for Bolton. He became interested in inventions and at first tried to solve the problem of perpetual motion. He returned to Preston in January 1768, along with an assistant called Kay who was a clockmaker. In the rooms provided by Henry he began to work on a device for the spinning of cotton. Such inventions were unpopular at the time, and he therefore announced that he was trying to create a machine for the finding of longitude. This would be a chronometer. The Government in 1713 had offered rewards of up to £20,000 for chronometers which could determine longitude within an error of 30 geographical miles. Such an instrument had, in fact, been produced by John Harrison in 1761, but the reward had not been paid. For Arkwright to say that he was seeking to produce such an instrument would therefore provide a good 'cover' for his real activities, and his employment of a clockmaker would lend colour to his story. In March 1768, while he was occupied with his invention, there was a Parliamentary election in Preston. The right to vote in such elections had been in doubt for some time. In 1661 the Mayor and Council claimed the right to elect members of Parliament without the involvement of the In-Burgesses, and accordingly appointed two members, The In-Burgesses held a poll and elected two other members. The matter was referred to the House of Commons which decided that all inhabitants of Preston had the right to vote. In 1768 the non-freemen resident in the town claimed the right to vote and elected General Burgoyne, and Sir Henry Hoghton, but the Mayor declared that Sir Peter Leicester, Bart and Sir Frank Standish, were elected. This led to a petition, and the rights of the electors were examined. The result was that all male inhabitants were declared to have the right to vote, which gave Preston the widest franchise in the country. (In Westminster all males except paupers could vote, but there was no such limitation in Preston.) The right of Arkwright to vote was challenged, and the following evidence was taken:

> 'Mr Henry – let him [Arkwright] some rooms in his house – has resided there since January at 7 guineas per annum, making a machine to find longitude. Apprehended he was a freeman when he let him the rooms – does not know why he apprehended so – rooms let till May come twelvemonth, acknowledged he had let it to Mr Parker till May next. Let it to Arkwright if Corporation should continue him tenant.
> John Kay – has known him twelve months – is a servant assisting him in making him a machine – his wife and children with him – his wife here five weeks ago, knows not where he came from but by stage from Manchester, working about a machine – knows not what it's for, but believes to find out longitude'.

Arkwright's right to vote was rejected – he would have voted for Leicester and Standish.

Because of Arkwright's occupation the building has ever since had his name attached to it. Some time later it became a public house called 'The Arkwright Arms', later again it became a lodging house, called 'Arkwright Arms Hostel', and it has since been rescued from decrepitude and converted into an Arts Centre.

Charles Hardwick in his *History of Preston* (page 651) states that the house occupied by Arkwright belonged to a Mr Smalley, that it was in Stonygate, and later became the Arkwright Arms. He is clearly wrong in this because Whittle, in the second volume of his *History of Preston* (page 215) mentions that Mr Smalley, a liquor merchant and painter joined Arkwright and Kay in business, and through his interest persuaded the Master of the Grammar School to grant them the use of a room, or back parlour attached to the house near the School for the making of the machine. He adds that the room was very secluded, and behind it was a garden filled with gooseberry trees. Two old women lived in a nearby thatched cottage, and said that they heard such strange noises of a humming nature, that they thought that the devil was tuning his bag-pipes, and that Arkwright and Kay were dancing a reel. This caused consternation in the locality. Whittle goes on to say that Arkwright was a freeman of the Borough, and was therefore entitled to vote. When canvassed by the candidates he said that his clothes were so ragged that he could not for shame go to the poll. A subscription was raised, and a complete outfit of clothes was purchased for him.

Robert Shepherd was still occupying the lower room of the School building, and on 31 December 1774 the Council fixed his rent at £5 per annum. However on 21 April 1777 the rent was reduced to £1 1s. 0d., but Shepherd was to keep the room in repair. On 11 October 1787 it was agreed that he should no longer pay rent, as the room was also being used as a Sunday School.

Chapter 6

Robert Harris, 1788–1835

WHEN Thomas Fleetwood died in 1788 the Rev. Robert Harris was elected Headmaster on 24 June. He was born at Clitheroe in 1764, and was a Bachelor of Divinity, and Fellow of Sidney Sussex College, Cambridge. He served as Headmaster for the longest period of any, not retiring until 1835 when he was seventy-one, having held the office for forty-seven years. In 1798 he became curate of St George's Church. In 1844 he became Vicar, when it became a separate parish, and he held this office until his death in 1862. He was the father of Edmund Robert Harris, the great benefactor both of the town, and of the School.

Harris's salary was £45 per annum, like Fleetwood's. It is interesting to note that another applicant for the post of Headmaster was Daniel Duff, of Kensington. He travelled to Preston for interview, and was allowed ten guineas expenses for the journey – nearly one quarter of the annual salary!

Harris was not a successful Headmaster – 'Battleaxe' in his history of the School published in the Preston Herald in 1894 sums the matter up – 'The history of the Grammar School under the supervision of Mr Harris is one of gradual decay, both the reputation of the School, and the number of scholars attending going down considerably.' Not long after his appointment a Committee was set up to consider school rules, and to report any necessary amendments. A possible result of this was the appointment of Thomas Knowles as Usher on 6 August 1790. (His predecessor, Thomas Jenkinson had been dismissed on 21 June 1788.) Nothing further seems to have been done until, on 23 October 1795, Harris applied to the Council to become an In-Burgess. His application was deferred, but the the Council passed the following resolution: 'Whereas the Free Grammar School of the Borough has very much declined of late years, and now only consists of a small number of scholars which is a considerable loss and inconvenience to the Borough, Ordered that the Mayor, Aldermen Grimshaw, Pedder, and James Pedder be appointed a Committee to enquire into the cause of the said decline, and convene before them Mr Harris the Headmaster and Mr Knowles the Usher of the said School for that purpose, and to make their report thereon, and also of such measures as shall seem to them necessary to be adopted for the future to restore the School to a proper state of credit and reputation, at the next meeting of the Council'.

Knowles must have left early in 1796, because on 11 March 1796 the

Town Clerk was ordered to advertise for a replacement in the *Cumberland Pacquet,* and in Manchester and Liverpool newspapers. The salary was to be £30 per annum plus perquisites and fire money (i.e. money to provide fuel to heat the classroom). Honour must have been satisfied because Harris was made an In-Burgess on 17 June 1796.

On 11 October 1804 the Town Clerk was asked to write to Harris telling him that on no account must he appoint an Usher without the approbation of the Council. On 1 April 1807 the Council agreed to submit a dutiful and loyal address to George III to express the members' approbation of his late firm, manly, and constitutional conduct, and Harris was appointed to prepare it. This, most probably, refers to the King's actions in respect of the Government's proposals to extend Catholic emancipation, which led to the Government resigning on 24 March 1807.

Rev. Robert Harris B.D., Headmaster, 1788–1835.

On 3 March 1812 the Committee was again instructed to enquire into the condition of the School, and was given power to act, but nothing further seems to have been done.

Whittle's *History* of 1821 (page 84) contains the following description of the School:

> The Grammar School of Preston is situated at Syke Hill, bottom of Stonygate, for teaching the higher branches of classical education, and is patronised by the Corporation, who pay the salaries to the Masters; and was probably founded by them. The Headmaster receives £45, and the Second Master £40 per annum. Mr B. Worthington left a field, or enclosure, for the benefit of the Headmaster, which is now built upon, and produces £50 per annum for ground rents. The school is open for boys from all parts, without restriction, except those boys who are not sons of freemen of the borough, who usually pay by the quarter, but this is now nearly extinct. Boys are admitted by the discretion of the Masters, about seven years of age, and are not liable to superannuation [i.e. are not required to leave at a particular age]. Number of scholars generally average forty. The present Masters are the Rev. Robert Harris, B.D. curate of St George's chapel, Headmaster, whose salary is in all £100 per annum, exclusive of the compliments paid him at Shrovetide, by the boys under his more particular care. The other parts of education are under the conduction of the Rev. John Harrison, curate of Grimsargh Chapel, and lecturer to the Penitentiary house in the town.

The Council was again unhappy with the state of the School, and on 28 January 1822 again appointed a Committee, consisting of the Mayor and the Aldermen, to enquire into the cause of the decay of the School, and to report to the next meeting. Harrison the Second Master had just retired on grounds of ill-health. On the 6 March the committee delivered a full report:

> It appears that at various former periods the scholars in the School have been so numerous as to require three masters; that in 1747, though the number of scholars was 65, the School was then considered to be in great decay; that at Christmas last there were only 13 scholars in the School, and that since that period there has been an increase of 4 or 5 boys; that the Rev. Robert Harris receives the following annual stipend exclusive of the salary as Keeper of Dr Shepherd's Library:
>
> | | |
> |---|---|
> | Rent arising from certain buildings erected on a field in Fishergate Lane | £54 |
> | From the funds of the Corporation | £45 |
> | The School House on a moderate computation worth | £35 |
> | | £134 |

That the late Under Master Mr Harrison (who through
declining health has recently resigned office) received
an annual stipend from the funds of the Corporation   £40
Giving a total of   £174

The Mayor and Council, having taken this report into their serious
consideration, it is agreed and ordered that independent of the discredit
which this inefficient state of the Free Grammar School has brought on
the Corporation, the trifling advantages which are derived by the Public
from it do not justify the expenditure of the before-mentioned annual
sum in its support, and they feel themselves called upon to make such
regulations and alterations for the government of the School as may tend
to restore it to respectability, but, as it has been stated that Mr Harrison's
late declining health, and want of exertion in his department, have operated
as the principle causes of the defective state of the School, and as a small
increase of scholars has taken place since Mr Harrison's resignation, the
Mayor and Council have determined for the present to adopt the following
temporary regulations by way of experiment. It is therefore agreed and
ordered that the Rev. Robert Harris be continued Headmaster of the said
School, and that Mr Peter Hoghton, who has been recommended to the
Mayor and Council by Mr Harris, and several other respectable clergymen,
and gentlemen, be appointed Usher of the said School in the room of
Mr Harrison, to hold the said several offices for the space of one year
from this day, subject to the will and pleasure of the Mayor and Council
to remove them, or either of them, at an earlier period if they shall see
occasion. That each of the Masters shall be allowed, during this his
temporary appointment, to receive through the hands of the Corporation's
Steward, and not otherwise, the rents and stipends hereinbefore mentioned
until the further order of the Mayor and Council. That Mr Peter Hoghton's
stipend after the rate of £40 to commence from the __ day of __ [sic]
last on which day Mr Harris, by mistake, and without the prior appointment of the Mayor and Council took him into the School as an assistant,
and at the expiration of the said year, or sooner if they see occasion the
Mayor and Council will, on consideration, make such further order upon
this subject respecting the future apportionment of the before-mentioned
rents and stipends or any of them, and the general establishment of the
School as they may deem proper, and as existing circumstances may
require. That in the meantime the gentlemen of the School Committee
are requested to continue their service until further order of the Council,
and, as soon as convenient, to form such Rules and Regulations for the
future good government of the School as they may see necessary, and
produce the same before the Mayor and Council at a future meeting,
and they are also requested from time to time to enquire into the state

of the said School, and the progress made by the scholars therein, and more specially to the commencement of the Holyday at Midsummer and Christmas in such manner as they shall think advisable, and, from time to time, to make their reports to the Mayor and Council, That a copy of this order be transmitted by the Town Clerk to the Rev. Mr Harris for the information of both, who, it is hoped will zealously co-operate with the Mayor and Council in their anxious endeavours to promote the increase, and utility of this ancient Grammar School.

After this momentous resolution no further action was taken by the Council for eight years.

The Charity Commissioners visited the School in 1823, and reported as follows:

There are no documents existing relative to the founding of the school, but as the Corporation seems to have had the management and control of it as far back as can be traced, it is probable that it was originally founded by them for the benefit of freemens' sons. In the old Corporation books there are entries from time to time from a very early period, ordering the School House to be repaired at the expense of the Corporation.

There is an excellent residence for the Headmaster and two good schoolrooms, one above, and one below. There is a Headmaster and Usher both appointed by the Corporation, and paid from their funds. The Headmaster receives salary of £45, and Usher or Undermaster £40.

These salaries have varied from time to time, and seem to be an entirely free gift from the corporation.

School and School House are in very good repair; the latter calculated to receive a small number of boarders. The premises are worth at least £30 per annum . . . [there follows a long description of the Worthington land, and its various lettings].

Income from the school field now £55 1s. 6d. received by the Head-master. In future vacancy some part should be paid to the Undermaster. When the Headmaster was appointed the rent was only £12.

School is open to sons of freemen without any charge. It is usual for parents to make compliments to the Headmaster at Shrovetide of half a guinea to two guineas. One guinea is the average.

For any boys coming from a distance the Master makes a charge according to his discretion.

No boarders at present. The Headmaster has declined them for four to five years. The Undermaster has no private pupils.

Present Headmaster has been 30 years in office and considers that the School is open to the sons of freemen without charge, and has adhered to that rule for some time.

Latterly no distinction except boarders.

In October 1823 [time of the enquiry] there were 36 boys all living with parents or relatives in Preston. 15 were in the upper school – strictly classical – not many go to University.

The Usher teaches the lower school reading and rudiments of grammar. He gets a cock-penny from the lower school. The Usher teaches writing and accounts at half a guinea a quarter each. These were taught 20 years ago by a teacher unconnected with the school. The lower schoolroom is let to another school at 6 guineas per annum. The low state of the School is the subject of complaint and regret amongst the inhabitants of Preston. We have received different statements as to the number of boys in the school during the early part of the time of the present Headmaster. It is however admitted that the number is now very considerably reduced though in the last two years there has been a small increase. It would be difficult to ascertain the precise reason for this reduction which must be imputed to various causes, but in all probability the ceasing to take boarders has had some effect.'

In Baines's *History of Lancashire* (1825, vol. 2, page 488) the same information is given. He states:

'Formerly the sons of freemen only were instructed gratuitously, others paying a quarterage, but this payment is not now exacted. The number of scholars varies from 30 to 40; the system of education is principally classical, but partly commercial. No exhibitions or other university advantages attach to this school, which is one reason why it has not produced many eminent men'.

He adds that the usher taught writing and accounts in the lower school for which two guineas a year was paid as quarterage.

A short description of the School at this period is contained in a letter sent to the Rev. H. C. Brooks, the then Headmaster, on 27 October 1900, by Mr Henry Oakey. The reason for the letter was that Brooks had written a short history of the School to place in a prospectus. Oakey said that he went to the School in 1822 or 1823. The boys of the Higher School, or Headmaster's side paid 7s. 6d. as a cock-penny, and the boys of the Lower Side 5s. 0d. In return three or four books were presented as prizes. They were not awarded for merit, but the recipients were selected by throwing dice – the boy with the highest throw had the first choice – Oakey considered that this was a more equitable method of awarding prizes! Fees for the High School were £4 or guineas, and for the Low School £2. There were 60 or 70 boys, later up to 100, and on one morning there were 105. The result was that the boys of other schools would not fight the Grammar School boys. Fires and lights had to be paid for – some had 'dips', and others thick wax candles. The cane was used on hands and shoulders. For more serious offences clothes were taken down and the victim was bent over a desk with feet and hands held. The birch was then applied to the bare skin – he only remembered this happening once.

The reminiscences of a man who must have been about ninety in 1900 are interesting, but not very reliable – he is obviously very wrong about the number of boys at the School in his time there.

On 12 September 1828 Peter Hoghton was given leave to attend Dublin and Oxford Universities, provided he found a competent person, approved by Harris, to fulfil his duties, and on 18 June 1830 he resigned.

The story of Peter Hoghton is unusual. After his death his memoirs were written by the Rev. R. Carus Wilson, Vicar of Preston, of which there is a copy in the Preston Library. He was born in 1802, and came of a good family. At the age of sixteen, in 1818, he was apprenticed to an attorney, but he indulged in a dissolute life, and ran away from home. He then became a private soldier in the 52nd Light Infantry (the Oxfordshire Regiment), but his health broke down, and he was invalided out in 1821. He returned home, became a reformed character, and began to study theology. He was appointed Usher in 1822, but in 1825 he went to Trinity College, Dublin, and obtained a BA degree in 1829. He was appointed curate at Walton-le-Dale, and on his resignation from the School went to Torquay, where he died of tuberculosis in 1830. How a number of respectable clergymen and gentlemen could consider that a young man of 20 who had led a dissolute life, and served as a private in the Army was a suitable Usher for the School is difficult to imagine. It is also difficult to see how he managed to attend University while carrying out his duties, and without the consent of the Council until 1828.

On 22 July 1830 William Harrison was appointed to replace Hoghton. At the same time the occupier of the lower school was given notice to quit, and the Committee issued new rules. These had been prepared without the concurrence of Harris, and he objected to some of them. On 26 November, after considering the objections, the Committee came to a final decision, and the new rules were agreed by the Council on 17 December. In the meantime, on 24 September a Committee of Visitors had been appointed.

The new rules can be summarized as follows:

1. The Headmaster was to teach boys of eleven and upwards, and the Usher was to teach English, Latin, Accounts, and Geography to the boys under eleven, but, with the Visitors' approval, the ages might be varied in individual cases. The Headmaster's scholars were to be taught Accounts by the Usher, subject to the Headmaster compensating him.

2. The Headmaster and Usher were to received a stipend of £45 each, and the Headmaster's scholars were to pay him one guinea per quarter,

and the Usher's fifteen shillings a quarter, but sons of freemen were only to pay one half of these sums, and the Masters could charge at a lower rate if they wished. No fire money, cock-pennies or other perquisites were to be received by the Masters.

3. Each Master was to devote the whole of the school hours to the School, and no officiating clergyman was to be elected in future.

4. Each Master must give a quarterly report to the Mayor.

5. The Committee, consisting of one alderman, and three councillors, was to visit the School monthly.

6. Each Master was liable to be dismissed, or to resign on six months notice.

7. Scholars to give one quarter's notice of leaving, or to pay one quarter's fees.

8. A Writing Master was to attend on such terms as the Corporation should fix.

9. Each scholar must provide his own books, paper, pens, ink, slates etc.

10. Holidays were to consist of one month at Midsummer, and one month at Christmas, and the School terms were to be printed and circulated by the Headmaster.

11. The Corporation would keep the School building, desks and forms in repair, but not the windows.

On 1 June 1831 the Committee of Visitors reported that, having received seven applications for the post of Writing Master, they had appointed Joseph Peppercorn of 21 Fox Street, who was to attend at the School from 11 a. m. to noon on Mondays, Tuesdays, Wednesdays and Fridays, and was to charge six shillings a quarter, and three shillings for the sons of freemen.

They had examined the school rooms, and found them so dilapidated as to render them unfit for a respectable Master or scholars to occupy. The Upper Room was therefore to be renovated immediately according to a plan and estimate that had been prepared.

They had also examined the toilet facilities and 'viewed a public and private nuisance belonging to the School, miscalled a "necessary"', and proposed that a proper and convenient one be built near the corner of a piece of land opposite the South wall of the National School, and to be appropriated solely for the use of the Grammar School.

On 20 June 1833 it was reported that there were now 45 boys attending, an increase of 13 since Harrison's appointment. In the Upper School there were 8 sons of freemen, and 10 others, and in the Lower School there were 14 sons of freemen and 13 others. Coals, cleaning etc. cost £5 and half was paid by each Master. 43 boys were having writing lessons, and there had been no complaints by parents.

By December 1833 the numbers had risen to 52. Everything was very satisfactory, except that many panes of glass had been wantonly broken, but not by the scholars. Harris was late with his report in June 1834, but a stove had been introduced which had reduced the dampness in the south-west wall, and a terrestrial globe had been lent by the Library. At the end of the year there were 45 or 46 boys.

On 22 April 1835 Harris submitted a letter stating that he intended to resign on 18 June 1835. He was 71, and said that he was retiring because of ill-health. He had suffered each winter for some years, and did not feel that at his age he could expect any improvement. Nevertheless he continued to hold the office of Vicar of St George's for another 27 years, dying at the age of 98 on 6 January 1862, having preached his last sermon on the previous Christmas Day.

Altogether it seems clear that the School, during Harris's time was in a most unsatisfactory state, and he appears to have neglected it for his ecclesiastical duties. He was very popular with his parishioners, and in 1834 received a large gift of silver plate from them (208 oz altogether). The Mayor and Council accepted his resignation with alacrity, and were probably glad to see him go. The great benefit that he conferred on the town was in having a son who provided, not only scholarships for the School, but public works and a great charity which still benefits the community as a whole. A bust of Harris is in the Museum, and his tomb is in St George's Church.

Chapter 7

The Move to Cross Street, 1835–1859

O N RECEIPT of Harris's resignation the Council at once appointed a Committee for the conduct and management of the School, and to consider what branches of education should be carried on therein, and by what Masters, and at what salaries and allowances.

On 22 May 1835 the Committee reported that Harris had been receiving £172 19s. od. per annum, and Harrison £120. Peppercorn was still the Writing Master. The teaching of Classics and Mathematics was sound, but no Modern Languages were taught. It was decided that, on the retirement of Harris, a Classical Tutor should be engaged who must be a graduate, and, if in Orders, must not be officiating. The Council should take over the Headmaster's House, which might be more valuable for commercial purposes, and the value of the House would provide a fund to pay an instructor of Modern Languages. The present site of the School was considered to be an obstacle because of the deterioration of the Stonygate area. If rebuilt on a better site more fees might be obtained. Generally the School should be put on the same basis as a proprietary school.

The Council approved the report, and asked the Committee to advertise for a Classical Tutor, and to report on the question of employing a Modern Language Tutor or Tutors. It was also resolved that the Council was willing to undertake the expense of rebuilding the School on an enlarged and improved plan.

On 26 May 1835 the Rev. George Nun Smith MA was appointed Headmaster during the pleasure of the Council. He came from Yoxford in Suffolk, and had been a Scholar of Sydney Sussex College, Cambridge. He was not to hold any living, incumbency, or curacy, or any permanent ecclesiastical duty.

The School must have closed when Harris left, for on 17 July 1835 it was decided that it would re-open on 27 July. The quarterly fee was to be 2 guineas, and would include French, Writing and Accounts. The fees were to be used to pay the salaries of the French Master, and the Writing Master, and the balance was to be divided between the Headmaster and the Second Master in a fixed proportion. The Headmaster's salary was guaranteed at £70, and the Second Master's at £50. School hours were to be from 9 a.m.

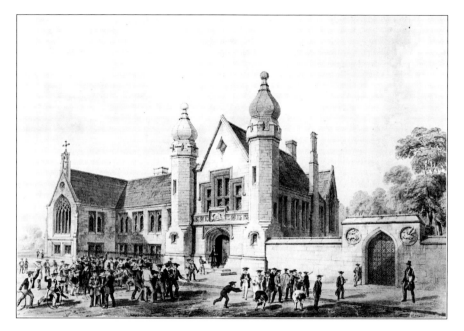

Preston Grammar School, Cross street, *c.* 1850, from a contemporary print.

to noon, and from 2 p.m. to 5 p.m., with half holidays on Wednesday and Saturday. A cleaner was to be engaged, and an advertisement for scholars was to be issued. The subjects were to be Latin, Greek, French, English Language and Literature, Writing, Mathematics and Arithmetic.

The half-yearly report in December showed that there were now 31 boys, but it was felt that the increase of the fees was causing a temporary diminution in new entrants. The fees had produced £124 7s. 0d. which had been divided up, the French Master receiving £21., the Writing Master £9 7s. 0d., the Headmaster £49 2s. 0d., and Harrison, the Second Master, £44 2s. 0d.

In 1835 the Municipal Corporations Act was passed, abolishing the old form of local government, and establishing new elective councils which took office on 1 January 1836. On the same day a new Grammar School Committee was appointed, and its first business was to consider the propriety of continuing the Masters' stipends, presumably on the grounds that they were getting sufficient from the fees, but in March the Committee decided to continue the stipends.

The School House was now standing empty and in August it was decided to make it fit for habitation. As mentioned earlier it became a public house called 'The Arkwright Arms'. Smith had occupied Avenham House, which was in a pleasanter position, and for which he paid himself.

On 23 February 1837 the Council decided that ten boys, who were sons of freemen, were to be admitted on payment of only 2 guineas per annum. Applications were to be made through the Committee, and thereafter, from time to time, boys were admitted under this system.

Smith applied to be allowed to take religious services on Sundays only, and, despite its previous decision, the Council agreed on 28 August 1838, and in 1841 went so far as to agree to him officiating in clerical functions, provided that there was no interference with the discharge of his regular duties in the School.

On 9 November 1839 the Rev. Edwin Smith BA of St John's College, Cambridge was appointed Second Master, he being the brother of the Headmaster, and in 1842 the first native French Master was appointed, a Monsieur Collas.

The Writing Master retired in 1841, and Smith asked the Committee for the appointment of a full-time Third Master to teach Writing, Mapping, Surveying and Mechanical Drawing. He was authorised to make an appointment, subject to the Committee's approbation.

Nothing had so far been done to implement the Council's decision to build a new School, but on 30 August 1841 the Committee was authorized to consult with the Headmaster. He had pointed out that the schoolroom was inadequate for the increased number of scholars, and that he was prepared, from his own resources, to erect a larger schoolroom on a better site upon a plan and elevation to be approved of by the Treasurer. To be able to do this he would need to be allowed to make a small addition to the fees (except of those of the ten boys nominated by the Council) so as to afford him a return on the proposed outlay.

It was resolved that the Committee be authorized to consent on behalf of the Council 'to the business of the School being conducted in such new schoolroom, and to fix the amount of such proposed increase in quarterage, this Council being willing that any rent arising from the present schoolroom should be paid to the proprietors of the new schoolroom till further orders by the Council, and if the property of such new schoolroom can be obtained by the Council upon terms approved of by them, the old schoolroom and school house may be sold and the produce applied in such purchase.'

It appears that the new School was not financed by Smith alone, but by a group of private shareholders. The share capital was £2,550, and money was also borrowed from Peddar & Co.'s Bank.

Once the approval of the Council had been obtained, a site was chosen to the south of Fishergate in Cross Street. The architect was John Welch, and he chose to design the building in what was called 'the Tudoresque style'. It was built of stone from Longridge.

Over the main door were the arms of the School (see Chapter 14) carved in stone, probably by William Duckett, who was the sculptor responsible for the statue of Sir Robert Peel in Winckley Square. Hardwick describes the building as follows:

> 'It is a handsome building in the Tudor style of architecture, and contains on the ground floor, a hall for recreation, sixty feet in length. The principal storey consists of a lofty open roofed hall for study, class room, and a transept, forty feet long. On the ground floor of the transept is the school-room, forty feet in length by twenty in width. The windows of the hall bear some resemblance to those of Merton College, Oxford'.

This description, coupled with the engraving (dated 1854), in Hardwick's *History* shows that the building was in the shape of a T, with the base of the upright in Cross Street. There was an imposing entrance up four steps, and at each side of the entrance were pillars with onion shaped capitals. On the easterly side was a gateway with carved roundels. This was removed in 1932, at the expense of the Preston Grammar School Association, and re-erected in Moor Park Avenue as a boys' entrance to the new school.

In 1845 another building was erected to the West of the School. This was named the 'Collegiate Library', and was used as a class-room for the senior boys. It was decorated with stained glass created by Ballantynes of Edinburgh. The Council allowed the fees for the senior boys to be raised by one guinea per annum to pay for this addition. The main hall of the school was 'elaborately ornamented with pictures in distemper, painted by Frank Howard, representing subjects from English history, interspersed with the decorative ornaments, mottoes etc.' These pictures were presented to the School by John Addison, the judge of the County Court at Clitheroe.

In fact the pictures were not painted in distemper on the wall, but were painted in oil on paper which was stuck on canvas, and the canvas was then fastened to battens affixed to the wall. We know this because on 23 November 1848 the artist, Frank Howard, presented a paper to the *Historical Society of Lancashire and Cheshire* (see *Transactions*, vol. 1, p. 30) in which he described the works in detail. He stated that the paintings were 'now putting up in the Grammar School, Preston', so it seems that it took some years for the work to be done. The following is a summary of his description:

1. The Grammar School was now rising in eminence and, in addition to the annual allowance by the Corporation, a subscription had been entered into by various gentlemen of the town and neighbourhood to place the School on a footing with the best Public Schools in the Kingdom.

2. Judge Addison had asked Howard to prepare a design for the decoration of the walls with paintings.

3. The School consisted of three rooms, called the Greek, Latin, and

English schools. These were to be used to illustrate Greek, Roman, and English history respectively.

4. The large gable end of the English school was 28 feet high above the wainscot, and 26 feet wide, and was to be devoted to English history from the Norman Conquest to the death of Elizabeth.

5. Various alterations were made to the scheme, but the final result was:

   (a) At the apex the introduction of Christianity to the North of England – Coifi the High Priest throwing his spear at the Saxon idols.

   (b) An upper series with round arches – in the centre Alfred the Great founding Oxford University, on one side Canute rebuking his courtiers, and on the other Henry II establishing the Flemish weavers.

   (c) A range of pointed arches containing – Richard I in the Holy Land, Constance of Britanny and Prince Arthur, John signing Magna Carta, Wycliffe, Chaucer, and Froissart, Henry III meeting the Armed Parliament, Edward III and Queen Philippa, and the Black Prince and King John of France.

   (d) A range of florid gothic arches containing – Wat Tyler and Richard II, Richard II taking leave of his Queen, the marriage of Henry V, the crowning of Henry VI in Paris, Humphrey Duke of Gloucester and Warwick the Kingmaker, the murder of Edward Prince of Wales after Tewkesbury, the murder of the Princes in the Tower, and the battle of Bosworth Field.

   (e) A range of Tudor arches containing – Henry VIII dismissing Wolsey, Edward VI and Bishop Ridley, Queen Mary releasing prisoners from the Tower, and Queen Elizabeth in Council.

Altogether it must have been a most impressive sight but there is no mention of Greek and Roman history being illustrated.

The condition of the pictures must have deteriorated, because in January 1892 it was decided by the Council that £20 should be spent on renovating them. It is not known what happened to them, no doubt they could not be transferred when the School moved to Moor Park. There was a lithograph of them in the Harris Art Gallery, but it can no longer be found. When the building was about to be demolished in 1957, Mr Paviere, the then Curator of the Art Gallery was asked to examine the walls, but this was because of the mistaken belief that the pictures had actually been painted on the walls.

There is a further description of the building in *A Handbook and Guide to Preston* written by William Pollard in 1882. He states that the frontage to Cross Street was about 100 feet long, extending to Guild Hall Street, with a frontage to that street of 70 feet. He goes on:

'At the west end of the Cross Street frontage there is a bold and prominent gable enclosing a lofty and handsome tracery window. Immediately to the west of this gable a flight of steps leads to an entrance into one of the large class rooms, which is on a higher level than the principal class room, approached from the main entrance. Eastward from the gable the elevation contains ranges of mullion windows. At the eastern boundary of the frontage the elevation has two octagonal towers between the arched and recessed entrance, above which is a three light mullion window, surmounted by a gable . . . The principal class room is used for prayer in the morning, before the commencement of the day's studies. At the north end of the room there are some well executed frescoes. Besides the two large class rooms already named there are also similar rooms in the basement portion of the building'.

All records say that the move to the new building was in 1841. It is difficult to see how this was possible when the approval of the Council was only given in August of that year.

The Headmaster now occupied Avenham House, which was about seven minutes walk from the new school. There was room here for boarders, but as the number increased it was necessary for an adjoining house to be taken over. Avenham House was not owned by the Corporation, but was the personal responsibility of the Headmaster.

In 1850 a school magazine was produced entitled *The Scholar*. It was published fortnightly at first, but then every three weeks. It had eight pages, and cost 2*d*. It did not last for very long, being suppressed by the Headmaster on the grounds that it was 'anarchical'.

More scholars must have been attracted because by 1854 the number had risen to 115, of which 10 were the sons of freemen. In November 1854 the Headmaster wrote to the Committee stating that for some time he had been suffering from deafness, which hindered his work. He had recently appointed Mr G. Heppell, BA (A Wrangler in 1853, and no relation to the present author), as an extra assistant, but he was now thinking of retiring, and would do so if the Council would offer him a reasonable pension. He suggested that his brother Edwin (who was now an MA) might be appointed in his place. The Committee was minded to agree to this, but refused to do so until Smith actually resigned. It then offered a pension of £100 per year. He accordingly resigned, and Edwin Smith took office, and Thomas Cox MA of St John's College, Cambridge, the Third Master was appointed to replace Edwin as Second Master on 1 February 1855.

Prior to these changes the Council published figures showing the financial situation. The cost of the School to the Corporation was £161 per annum, made up of a payment to the Headmaster of £100, a payment to the Second Master of £45, and the cost of cleaning and firing of £16. The income from the Worthington land was £55 3s., so that the net cost to the Corporation was £105 1s. It is clear from this that the Headmaster no longer received the money from the land directly. It was no longer a free school. There were 9 scholars upon the foundation, who paid to the Masters two guineas per year. There were 91 scholars not on the foundation who paid eight guineas per year to the Masters, plus two guineas per year towards the rent of the buildings if they were in the 1st and 2nd classes, and one guinea if they were in other classes. From this it appears that the Masters shared over £783.

On 1 January 1856 Edwin Smith reported on the half-year ending in December 1855. There were 85 boys, of whom 5 had been recommended by the Council, and 2 boys were being paid for by the Masters.

It seems that the Council was finding difficulty in nominating the sons of freemen, and on 4 December 1856 it was decided to include the sons of non-freemen in the ten places to be nominated. The object of this was said to be to give an opportunity for the more meritorious boys trained in the diocesan, national, and commercial schools in the town to receive a grammar school education. This decision was adhered to for a time, but thereafter for some years only the sons of freemen were appointed.

The Headmaster's next report in January 1857 was as follows:

The number of Scholars who attended at the Grammar School during the half-year ending Christmas 1856 amounted to 72; five of whom were admitted on the recommendation of the Corporation. The subjects which have engaged the attention of the pupils have been portions of Euripides, Xenophon, the Holy Scriptures in Greek and English, Tacitus, Virgil, Ovid, Caesar, Cornelius Nepos, and the elementary books which are usually read in Grammar Schools. The study of the Modern Languages, as well as that of Geography, Chemistry, and of the Histories of Rome and England, has formed a part of the usual routine. The subjects of instruction in Mathematics have been Conic Sections, Trigonometry, Algebra, Euclid, Statics, and Arithmetic. Some of the Mechanical, and other drawings produced during the half-year have been very creditable.

This is a formidable list, surprising because of the absence of Homer, and Cicero, and the presence of Cornelius Nepos.

In the same year the old school building in Stonygate was demolished, and shops were built on the site.

On 18 June 1857 the Mayor visited the School to present prizes. He went in full robes, attended by the Corporation maces, and with many members of the Council. This seems to be the first record of this ceremony, which became an annual event. Mr E. G. Hancock, Fellow of St John's College, Cambridge, had examined the boys, and gave his report, which was a very satisfactory one. He particularly referred to Myers, the School Captain, who was leaving to go to University. He later became Vicar of St Paul's Church, Preston, and was the father of Sir J. L. Myers, referred to later (see Chapter 17). Prizes were then presented. The Mayor gave prizes for Scripture History, and Profane History, and prizes were also given by the Town Clerk, and the Headmaster. The staff consisted of the Headmaster; the Rev. T. Cox, MA, Second Master; Mr F. Exton, BA, Third Master; Mr Tuke, Fourth Master; Monsieur Loewe, French and German Master; and Herr Loth, Drawing Master.

The Committee received a letter of resignation from Edwin Smith on 9 October 1857, stating that he had been appointed an Assistant Chaplain to the Forces, and he left on 1 December 1857. He died on 9 April 1871.

A Sub-Committee was set up to consider what should be done, and enquiries were made from other towns with grammar schools. The reason for this was probably concern at the fact that numbers at the School were again declining. Advertisements for a new Headmaster were published in the *Cambridge Chronicle,* the *Oxford Herald,* and *The Times*. It was decided that the School should be divided into Upper and Lower Schools. The Upper School subjects were to be Divinity, Latin, Greek, Mathematics, Arithmetic, French, German, Drawing, History, Geography, English Composition, Natural Philosophy, and Writing. Greek, German and Drawing were to be optional. The Lower School subjects were to be the same with the exclusion of Greek and Natural Philosophy, and the addition of Natural History and Book-keeping, with German and Drawing optional. Fees were to be 10 guineas per year for the Upper School, and for the Lower School 7 guineas, and 6 guineas for those under 10. Sons of freemen were to pay 2 guineas per year for the Upper School, and all were to pay 2 guineas a year for German, and 1 guinea for Drawing. The fees for boys already at the School were not to be increased. At that time there were 60 boys at the School, of whom 12 were sons of freemen, and it was calculated that the fees to be received by the Headmaster would be £300. If numbers increased to 70 fees would be £340, and if to 80 they would be £400. This calculation took no account of the fees received from boarders. The Headmaster's salary was again to be £100, and the Second Master was to receive, in addition to his salary of £45 from the Corporation, the sum of 1½ guineas per boy from the Headmaster.

Twenty-three applications were received, and the Rev. Howson, Principal of the Liverpool Collegiate Institute was asked to help in the selection. A short list was prepared, and one candidate, the Rev. Lonsdale Pritt withdrew because he had 'ascertained certain facts which made it his duty to consider the matter very carefully'. He thought that another candidate, the Rev. John Richard Blakiston, MA was a better man. In fact the Committee agreed with him and recommended the appointment of Blakiston to the Council. He was from Trinity College Cambridge, and was First Assistant Master at Uppingham. When the recommendation came to the Council on 1 January 1858 there was a debate on the matter, and a resolution was proposed and seconded that the Rev. T. Cox, the Second Master, be appointed Headmaster instead of Blakiston. The resolution was lost by 14 votes to 27, and the Committee's recommendation was approved.

In the meantime the Committee had become concerned about the position of Cox, and he was asked if he wished to continue as Second Master. He replied that he would consider, but pointed out that by the terms of his appointment he was entitled, not to 1½ guineas per pupil, but to two-fifths of the fees. He was then asked, in a letter from the Town Clerk, whether it was true that he was setting up a private school of his own, and was soliciting pupils at the Grammar School to transfer to his school. He declined to reply until he knew under what terms the allegations had been made. The Committee then decided to ask the Council to declare the post of Second Master vacant, and that Cox accordingly be dismissed. This the Council did at the meeting on 1 January, and also resolved that in future the Second Master was to be appointed by the Headmaster at the usual salary of £45, and that his share of the fees was to be agreed between them. Cox then wrote on 6 January denying the right of the Council to deprive him of his office. The Council rescinded the resolution dismissing him, and resolved that the appointment and removal of the Second Master was now a matter for the Headmaster. It appears that Blakiston must have exercised his new power since Cox left, and opened his own private school, and Arthur Brewin was appointed Master of the Lower School on 28 January.

The income of Blakiston was assured by the Committee agreeing, on 6 January, to guarantee to make up the amount of the fees to £300 per year, and at the same time it was decided to advertise that the School would re-open on 28 January, and that it would be conducted on a new plan calculated to meet the wants of a far wider circle than heretofore, and particularly to prepare boys for the Universities, the Army and the Navy. Boarders were to be taken, the Upper School in the Headmaster's House, and the Lower School in the Second Master's House. Boarding fees were to be £45, and £35 respectively, exclusive of tuition.

In February 1858 the Council thanked the former Headmaster The Rev. George Nun Smith for a gift of mechanical models.

The advent of Blakiston does not seem to have caused a resurgence in the School, for it was agreed that, although there would be the usual prize-giving ceremony, there was to be no 'Public Day' at Midsummer. There was also a reduction in boarding fees for seniors to 40 guineas, and Drilling and Singing were to be added to the curriculum. Brewin left in

October, and was replaced by Christopher Smith. Towards the end of the year Blakiston suggested that the fees should be changed because they provided a 'premium on backwardness'. In other words older boys who did not work hard enough to get into the Upper School were charged lower fees than those who succeeded. It was also ascertained that the income from fees for the year had amounted to only £180 6s. 3d., so that the Council was obliged to pay Blakiston £119 13s. 9d. to make up his income from fees to the agreed sum of £300. It was then decided that in future the guarantee was to be limited to £120, and that if the Headmaster left before the end of 1859 the guarantee for that year would be void. The Committee also asked for a copy of the School Rules. On 9 December 1858 Blakiston replied. He did not provide a copy of the Rules, but said that they were the same as those at Public Schools, and that some of the most important were not being complied with, and that he was tightening them, particularly those relating to absence.

It was obvious that Blakiston had not been a success, and had not been happy at the School, and on 4 January 1859 he wrote (from Mobberley Hall) stating that he had been elected Headmaster of Giggleswick School, and would be leaving Preston at once.

The Committee met on 7 January, and decided to make changes – the division into Upper and Lower Schools was to be abolished, and Commercial and Mathematical elements were to be made more prominent. The new tuition fees were to be 6 guineas for boys under 12, and 8 guineas for those of 12 and upwards. Extras were to be German, French and Drawing, and 1 guinea per year was to be paid for each. Sons of freemen were still to pay 2 guineas, plus extras. This change put into effect the suggestion of Blakiston, because fees were now to be fixed by the age of the pupil, and not by his position in the School.

An advertisement for a new Headmaster was at once issued, and 27 applications were received. On 26 January the Rev. William Caldicott, MA of Oxford was appointed. However he had hardly taken up his appointment when, on 2 April 1859, he wrote to say that he had been appointed Public Examiner in the University of Oxford, and felt that he could not continue at the School. He therefore resigned. He later became Headmaster of Bristol Grammar School, and Rector of Shipston-on-Stour. He died in 1895.

In conclusion, there are two stories about the Smith brothers: As already mentioned Nun Smith, towards the end of his service, became very deaf. One day when he was receiving fees from the boys, he asked one how his father was. The boy replied that his father had been dead for nine months. Smith did not hear a word, but replied, 'I'm very glad to hear it!'

When Edwin Smith was Headmaster the boys of the boarders' house were in the habit, at night, of lowering one of their number out of a bedroom window on a sheet, so that he could go and buy sweets for them. Smith lurked in the bushes, and saw this going on. The next night, when the signal to haul up the boy with the sweets was given, they found that he seemed to have gained in weight, and there was consternation when they found that they had hauled up their Headmaster.

Chapter 8

G. T. Tatham, 1859–1874

THE COMMITTEE again advertised for a Headmaster, and this time received no less that 78 applications. On 20 May 1859 the Rev. George Turner Tatham, BA, Scholar of St John's College Cambridge was appointed. He had been educated at Sedbergh Grammar School, was 27 years of age, unmarried, and had been Assistant Master at Bromsgrove Grammar School. Unlike his immediate predecessors he stayed for 14 years. He found the School in a very sorry condition. On his arrival there were only 19 boys, but numbers increased during his Headmastership to a maximum of 158 in 1873.

During the interregnum the Second Master had been in charge, and on 1 June 1859 he was awarded £25 for his extra services.

In October 1859 fees were again changed. Boys under 10 were to pay 6 guineas, those under 12 – 8 guineas, and those 12 and over – 10 guineas. German, French and Drawing were extras at 2 guineas each, and sons of freemen, as before, paid 2 guineas. It seems that all was not well with the school buildings because it was agreed that temporary repairs should be carried out, and the Town Clerk was instructed to obtain a list of the shareholders. The result of this was that on 6 January 1860 Mr Philip Park, and Mr I. B. Dickson called on the Town Clerk to ask if the Corporation was prepared to buy or rent the school buildings. The school yard was subject to a ground rent of £10 per annum, and the shareholders owed £350 to Pedders Bank, plus interest from June 1859. The Committee offered to be responsible for the ground rent, the loan, and the interest, and to pay £850. The proprietors held a meeting, and decided that the building should be sold. One of the proprietors had recently died, and his shares had been sold by public auction, and had realised one third of their face value. As the total share capital was £2550, the result of the auction placed a value of £977 10s. 0d. on the whole, and the proprietors offered to sell for this amount, subject to the loan liability. To this the Council agreed, and the conveyance was laid before the Council on 9 July 1860. The actual amount paid was £1,347 10s. 0d. In some of the local histories other figures are given, but this is the figure recorded in the Minutes.

At the same time a report on the heating and lighting of the buildings was called for, and this resulted in £68 being spent on a heating system, and the installation of gas lighting.

There was a number of small municipal charities provided for the binding of poor children as apprentices. These had been established by George Rogerson in 1619, Henry Banester in 1642, Thomas Winckley in 1720, and Henry and Eleanor Rishton in 1738. Of late years there had been no applicants for any of these charities, and on 26 July 1860 the Council decided to ask the Charity Commissioners to appropriate the funds to provide scholarships or exhibitions at the School. Consideration of this matter took time, and it was not until April 1865 that the Charity Commissioners finally approved a scheme. The money from the old charities consisted of: a rent of £9, a moiety of a rent of £16, £829 2s. 2d. in cash, a moiety of £313 14s. 6d. and £63 10s. 3d. in the Three per cents. It was expected to produce £56 17s. 3d. per year, and the Council wished there to be an exhibition of £30 per year, and 3 scholarships of £10 per year. The exhibition would have been for an ex-pupil attending university. However the approved scheme was for 6 scholarships at the School, each of £10 per year. No doubt the Commissioners considered that a university exhibition was not close enough to the original intention of the founders of the charities.

Tatham seems to have been successful from the start, and did not trouble the Committee for the first year – the only important resolution in 1861 being to increase the cleaning woman's wage from 4 shillings a week to 6 shillings! His success is evidenced by the fact that when the Second Master left in February 1862 to take up an appointment as Principal of the Scottish Episcopal Training College at Edinburgh, he was able to say in his letter of resignation that he was pleased to leave at the height of the School's prosperity.

Tatham suggested to the Committee that it might aid recruitment to the vacant post if the Bishop (of Manchester in those days) would agree to offer ordination to the successful candidate. The Committee thought this to be a good idea, and an Alderman was requested to wait upon the Bishop to obtain his views. The Bishop was complaisant, subject to the proviso that if he ordained a Second Master, the Council would not dismiss him without the Bishop's agreement.

On 16 April 1863 the Headmaster reported that there were now 104 boys in the School. A piece of land behind the building was rented as a playground for £15 per annum, and was gravelled for £6.

In November the Headmaster reported that there were still 104 boys, but that, as a result of the depressed state of trade, many were leaving early, or not starting at the School at all. It must be remembered that this was at the height of the Cotton Famine caused by the American Civil War, and the closure of the cotton mills affected the whole of the town's economy. He also commented that some boys entered the School too late – at 14 or 15. There were now 7 Masters in all, 4 Assistants, 1 Foreign Master, and a Drawing Master.

On 30 March 1864, Tatham attended the Committee, and submitted a most important proposal. He explained that late entrance was a problem – in the last two years boys of 18 had entered for the first time, and the average age of entry was 13. Moreover these late-comers had not received sufficient education before entering the School to benefit, and only stayed 2 to 2½ years, since the average age of leaving was 15 to 16. He therefore proposed that a Preparatory School should be founded under the patronage of the Corporation, which would provide, in due course, a number of boys already well prepared to enter the main school. He would superintend the Preparatory School himself, and it would be kept entirely separate from the main School, and would be accommodated in Avenham House. Ages would be from 6 to 10, but pupils might enter the main School at 8½ to 9. Subjects would be English, Writing, Arithmetic, Rudiments of Latin, and French. Fees would be 4 guineas under 8, and 6 guineas 8 and over. The Headmaster would derive no financial benefit from the scheme, because the fees would only be sufficient to pay the necessary extra Master.

The Committee accepted the proposal, subject to the sons of freemen being admitted on payment of 2 guineas, as in the main School, and a prospectus was duly prepared.

The Preparatory School was a success, and by 1870 there were 55 boys attending it. Avenham House soon became too small, and a move had to be made to the lower rooms of the main School in 1869. A photograph taken in 1871 shows Tatham and the boys of the Preparatory School. He was an imposing figure with a long and luxuriant black beard. He looks, and was, a strict disciplinarian, and like most Headmasters of his day indulged in public flogging.

A number of boys attended the Preparatory School without intending to proceed to the main School, but instead went on to Public Schools. One of these was Lieutenant-General Sir Percy Lake, born in 1855, who attended for a few years, and then went on to Uppingham (see Chapter 17).

In November 1864 the scholars applied for the honour of being allowed to march in the Mayor's procession to the Parish Church on Mayor's Sunday. Permission was granted, and this became an annual event, although in later years, when numbers had increased, it was only the prefects who marched.

From Midsummer 1865 it became the custom to print the report of the Examiner, who visited the School each year, and to include details of fees etc. A Drill Master had now been employed, namely ex-Sergeant Scott. Terms for boarders were 45 guineas if aged under 12, and 50 guineas if aged 12 or over, but this included tuition, and there were no fees for extra subjects. However, like the Mock Turtle's School, Washing was extra – 4 guineas. There were also 'day boarders' who were charged 23 and 25 guineas. They presumably travelled a long distance – there were boys from

Lytham and Blackpool. Preparatory fees for boarders were 40 guineas, but this included Washing, and day boarders paid 19 guineas.

In February 1866 there were 34 boys in the Preparatory School, and 87 in the main School, and it was decided to try to acquire the building of the Literary and Philosophical Society adjoining the School. It was bought in 1867 for £1,527 10s. 0d. The history of this building is not clear. It is said to have been built to house the Shepherd Library, but was never used for that purpose, and Hardwick, writing in 1857 states that it was already used by the School at that time.

A report on the condition of the School in June 1866 stated that the walls and woodwork were very dirty, not having been decorated for 7 years, and the pictures (described in the report as 'cartoons') needed dusting. Redecoration was therefore authorised, and it was ordered that tablets should be put up showing the names of those granted the Miller Exhibition (see Chapter 15) and the scholarships. Later tablets were put up for other awards. They were painted black with the names in gold, and were moved to the Moor Park School when Cross Street was abandoned.

In 1867 the School was visited by a Mr Bryce on behalf of the Schools Inquiry Commission. He noted the fees charged, and the salaries paid, and stated that the Second Master's salary was now £65. He reported that the educational condition of the School was satisfactory, and in many points highly creditable considering the short tenure of the Headmaster. He noted that only 26 boys learned Greek, and that the larger part of the School formed what was practically a modern side. Further to this point, in 1870 Tatham issued a prospectus which stated that a Commercial Department had been established, the members of which did not learn Latin or Greek.

At the end of 1869 the Headmaster was asked to analyse those attending and produced the following figures:

	Main School	Preparatory School
Boarders	17	6
Boys from Preston	54	42
Boys from near Preston	8	2
Boy from Lytham	1	—
Boy from Blackpool	1	—
Sons of freemen	8	4
	89	54
Grand total		143

These figures must have set the members of the Committee thinking, because in June 1871 an important step was taken when the privilege of the sons of freeman to be admitted at the fee of 2 Guineas was abolished. To replace it a new scholarship scheme was introduced. There were to be 12 free scholarships, 3 to be granted each year, and each to last for 4 years. These were to be awarded to boys aged 12 and under, the awards to be based on the result of examinations held each year. The subjects were to be: Scripture, History and Knowledge, Geography, English History, English Grammar (Analysis and Parsing), Reading, Writing, Arithmetic, and Dictation. To compensate the Headmaster for the loss of fees he was to be paid 4 guineas for each scholarship holder.

The Committee members began to search for money to pay for scholarships, and in August 1871 the Town Clerk wrote to the Endowed Schools Commissioners describing the present position, and stating the Council's desire to improve the School. He mentioned that in Penwortham there was an educational charity called Walton's Charity which had an income of about £1,000 per year, and which could well be used in Preston. The cost of the scheme that was suggested was to be about £1,200 per year. As a result of this Mr D. R. Fearon, an Assistant Commissioner came to talk to the Committee, and to inspect the School in January 1873, but nothing seems to have come of the proposal.

Tatham's health suffered a breakdown, and on 15 April 1874 he submitted a letter of resignation, which was accepted with regret, and with a resolution thanking him for his great work for the School. When he took over in 1859 there were 19 scholars, and when he resigned there were 95 in the main School, and 47 in the Preparatory Department. He became Vicar of Leek, and died on 17 December 1893, aged 61.

Chapter 9

A. Beaven Beaven, 1874–1898

O<small>N 11 JUNE</small> 1874 Alfred Beaven Beaven MA of Pembroke College, Cambridge was appointed Headmaster to replace Tatham – there had been 51 applicants. He was the son of John Beaven of Redland, Bristol, was 28 years of age, married, but with no children. He was not, on appointment, in Holy Orders, but was soon ordained. Some confusion has been caused as to his name because Fishwick in his History gives the name as 'Beaver Beaver', and Leach in the Victoria County History makes the same mistake, no doubt following Fishwick.

Shortly after his appointment the Committee decided to have the School repainted at a cost of £70, and, at the same time to build new water closets, which were badly needed. These were to be built in the School yard, but, at the request of the Mayor, building was delayed so that negotiations could take place with the Public Hall Company, which wished to exchange some land with the School. This was in August 1874, but it was not until August 1879 that the water closets were at last built. One wonders how the boys managed during the intervening 5 years!

In December 1874 the Headmaster decided to alter the timetable. Hitherto the year had been divided into quarters, but he decided to follow what had become common practice, and to divide the year into 3 terms. He proposed that there should be 4½ weeks holiday at Christmas, 2 weeks at Easter, and 6½ weeks at Midsummer, i.e. 20 July to 2 September. He issued a circular, containing these proposals, to all parents, and included a form for them to return to show whether or not they agreed with the new system. They approved of the change, 63 being in favour, none against, and 17 being neutral.

In April 1878 an Alderman submitted a resolution to found a Commercial Department at the School (presumably that founded by Tatham had not been continued). This was rejected, but the Council asked for the matter to be considered, and, at the same time it was decided to provide three further scholarships for boys from elementary schools.

At this time Guildhall Street was being built by Myers Park and Co., and a dispute arose because of earth being dumped on the boundary of the School yard. The Town Clerk was instructed to start legal proceedings, but in 1879 the matter was amicably settled, and the School yard was surrounded by a wall.

In December 1879 the Harris bequest was received, consisting of £3,000 to provide scholarships. The Harris Trustees had control of a large sum of money under the will of Edmund Robert Harris (he was, of course, the son of Robert Harris the former Headmaster), and the Council considered that the time was ripe to provide a house for the Headmaster, and to considerably improve the School. It therefore requested the Trustees for a further grant of no less than £30,000. After considering this the Trustees replied that Harris had shown a desire to benefit the School, and had decided that £3,000 was the appropriate amount. The request for £30,000 was therefore refused.

At the Guild of 1882 it was decreed that the Headmaster, and the boys were to march in the Mayor's Guild procession. Thereafter the Headmaster, and the Head Scholar were to deliver Latin orations to which the Recorder was to reply. This was a revival of an old tradition. It was also in this year that the Council seems first to have concerned itself with the provision of some sporting facilities, and a sub-committee was set up to find a cricket ground. (For more details of this see Chapter 16.)

In 1883 a Harris Scholarship was awarded to a boy named William Fisher, but, most unusually, he resigned the emoluments because he was already receiving £130 in scholarships, and considered that this was enough, and that someone else should have the benefit of the Harris Scholarship. It was therefore awarded to Charles Lambert Pimblett.

Changes in the free entrance scholarship scheme were made in 1885. There were to be 3 further scholarships, each for 3 years, and they were to be available to all boys not exceeding 11 years of age, including boys in the Preparatory and Junior Departments. The subjects of the examination were to be: Reading, Writing, Elementary Mathematics, English History, Geography, English Grammar, Historical Books of the Old and New Testaments, and, if desired, rudiments of Latin and French. The Committee reserved the right to refuse to grant a scholarship to a successful candidate if it considered that his parents could afford to pay the fees. Not surprisingly few boys applied to take the examination, and of those who did few succeeded. For example, in 1887 3 boys applied for 2 scholarships, but only one was granted, and later in the same year two who passed the examination were found not to be eligible on grounds of age, and no scholarships were granted. As a result of this the Preston and District Teachers Association asked to send a deputation to meet the Committee, but the result of the meeting is not recorded.

In 1888 the question of Modern and Commercial education was again raised. It is clear that some of the members of the Committee were doubtful of the advantages of a Classical education, and wanted more practical subjects to be taught. Beaven submitted details of the present charges: 10 guineas per year for those aged over 12, 8 guineas for those aged 10 to 12, 6 guineas for those aged 8 to 10, and 4 guineas for those aged under 8. Extras were Modern Languages – 2 guineas, Drawing and Geometry the same, Drawing

1. Rev. A. B. Beaven MA, Headmaster 1874–98;
2. Rev. H. C. Brooks MA, Headmaster 1898–1911;
3. Rev. F. E. Brown MA, Headmaster 1911;
4. Rev. N. Trewby MA, Headmaster 1912–26;
from the *Old Boys' Magazine*, 1913 (copy in Harris Reference Library).

materials – 10*s*. 0*d*., Chemistry – 10*s*. 0*d*., stationery – 15*s*. 0*d*., and 17*s*. 6*d*. The Committee gave instructions that enquiries should be made from other similar schools, and that a Sub-Committee be formed to consider the matter. Beaven took it upon himself to change the curriculum, and in February 1890 reported that since January 1889 Book-keeping and Shorthand had been taught to boys not taking Greek, together with lessons on Commercial Terms, both in English and French. Only one period per day was allocated to Latin, and only 14 boys were taking Greek. This seems to have satisfied the commercially minded members of the Committee for the time being.

Beaven reported to the Committee the results of the various examinations taken, and they seem to have been very satisfactory. It is particularly interesting to note that two boys – H. C. Beaven, and C. L. Beaven did extremely well– both were in turn the youngest boys to pass the Oxford Local Examinations, and H. C. Beaven won a Mathematical Scholarship to Rugby. It must be assumed that they were the sons of the Headmaster.

Despite good examination results the School was in rapid decline during the last years of Beaven's Headmastership. This is best proved by the following table showing the number of scholars attending:

1882	137	1890	86
1883	133	1891	83
1884	125	1892	74
1885	111	1893	76
1886	102	1894	70
1887	108	1895	59
1888	98	1896	56
1889	92	1897	48
		1898	32

Why the School declined in this way it is difficult to say, but the blame must lie with Beaven himself. The Committee was, of course, aware of what was happening, and on 25 June 1894 the Chairman, and Councillor Park were requested to confer with Beaven with a view to improving the School. On 23 August Beaven submitted a report, and on 21 September Park resigned, and was replaced by the Mayor and two other members. Nothing seems to have resulted, and the Sub-Committee was dissolved in January 1895. In July of that year the general question affecting the present and prospective position of the School was considered. It was resolved that 'consideration of the matter relating to the present holder of the office of Headmaster be deferred for twelve months', which looks as if a warning had been issued to Beaven, and that he had been given a year to improve. The Committee went on to consider plans for re-arrangement of the School and appointed a Sub-Committee to consider whether anything could be done towards the sale of the present buildings with a view to a new school being provided on a more suitable site. Again nothing seems to have resulted from this, and in February 1897 a letter was received from the Rev. B. Nightingale, on behalf of the Preston Non-Conformist Council complaining of the condition of the School. The unpopularity of the School was further shown in March when only 3 boys applied to take the examination for 2 available scholarships (the number had been increased from 3 to 5 in 1895), and not one was considered fit to receive a scholarship.

Also in March 1897 consideration was given to providing a Chemistry laboratory, but before anything was done a letter was received in July from the Harris Institute offering to provide Chemistry lessons at the Institute for a class of not less than 12 boys, and not more than 25. In November another letter was received from the Harris Institute stating that it was proposed to set up a Modern School to teach: English, French, History, Geography, Mathematics, Chemistry, Physics, Drawing, Short-hand, Book-keeping, Wood and Metal work, and possibly Latin and German. Fees were to be £1 10s. 0d. per term, thus considerably under-cutting the School. The views of the Council were requested upon this proposal. On 6 December a Sub-Committee met representatives of the Institute, and stated that the proposed school would clearly satisfy a public need, and that the Council therefore would have no objection. The new school would however interfere with the Grammar School under present conditions, but the time had arrived for the Council to deal with the Grammar School with a view to improvement.

The result of this decision was that Beaven at last resigned – no doubt pressure was put upon him. He was only 52, and in his somewhat pitiful letter of resignation he pointed out that he had been unable to make provision for the future necessities of himself and family. He had been without boarders for many years, and at any time the numbers had been insignificant. He had maintained good examination results, and after his 24 years of service he felt entitled to some means of recognition. In June the Committee recommended that a sum of £250 be placed in the hands of trustees to expend for the benefit of Beaven's family – a most odd resolution. However the Council must have considered that Beaven was no longer worthy of recognition, and the recommendation was not approved.

Beaven stayed on to the end of the Summer term, and, no doubt as an act of justification, published printed details of all examination successes from 1874 to 1898.

Sir Charles Holmes, sometime Director of the National Gallery, published his autobiography in 1936. He was a boarder at the School for six months in 1880, and he describes Beaven:

The Headmaster of the Preston Grammar School, the Reverend Alfred Beaven Beaven, once, it was rumoured, had preached. But he had started his sermon with the phrase 'seated in your pews like stalled oxen', and the simile had proved too much for a prosperous middle-class congregation. His help thenceforth was confined to reading the Lessons. With his dark beard, beetling brow, eyeglass screwed tight into his right eye, and his reputation for flogging, Mr Beaven was a memorable figure as he poised himself two yards back from the lectern and turned the doings of Elijah and Ahab into dramatic reality. He had indeed something of the look and temper of a minatory prophet, coloured by the disdain of the scholar for the stolid citizens among whom his lot was cast.

Holmes goes on to say that there were less than a dozen boarders, in accommodation designed for over 40, and about 100 day boys at that time. The boys were worked very hard, and the examination results were good, but numbers were obviously declining, no doubt because of Beaven's methods. In the Mathematics class boys were stood in a crescent with their exercise books. The Master walked behind them armed with a cane, and examined their work. For each mistake he gave them a cut with the cane. Holmes got into trouble by saying that he had completed a French exercise when he had not done so. He was sent to the Headmaster and was to receive 10 cuts for lying. He was extended over a desk, and after receiving 6 strokes, and feeling what he described as 'unbearable agony', he promised never to lie again if he could be excused the remaining 4 strokes. Beaven said 'that hardly bears on the present case. Go down again', and with something like a chuckle gave him 4 more strokes. Later Holmes was pleased that his offer to remain truthful in future had not been accepted.

A prospectus exists which was issued by Beaven in which he states that he came second in the Indian Civil Service Examination in 1868, which shows great scholastic excellence, but there is no explanation as to why he did not avail himself of the opportunity of going to India. The fees are similar to those charged by Tatham, and there is a statement that school caps are only to be obtained from J. S. Walker and Sons of Fishergate. This seems to indicate that school caps of a modern pattern were in use instead of the college caps (or mortar-boards) which had previously been worn.

Beaven was a scholar of some note – when Professor J. A. R. Marriott published his book *The Remaking of Modern Europe* he mentioned in the Introduction that Beaven had read the proofs of the latter part of the book, and Norman Hodgson, a later Headmaster, said of him 'Although he published little or nothing, he was recognized in the world of scholarship as an authority upon whose amazing memory and meticulous accuracy other scholars could rely. I have often heard verbal testimonies to his qualities'.

On the day of Beaven's resignation the Committee received a report from the Sub-Committee to the effect that a new Headmaster should be appointed on the same pay and conditions, that the School buildings were adequate,

Arkwright House, the former Headmaster's house, erected in Stoneygate in the early eighteenth century (photograph of an original watercolour by Edmund Beattie, by courtesy of the Harris Museum and Art Gallery).

North front of the School from Moor Park Avenue
(photograph courtesy of C. Williams).

Part of the Memorial Window for the 1914–18 War in the School Hall, showing the Arms of the Borough of Preton and a portrait of John Colet and Helen Hoghton (photograph courtesy of ABC Videos, Preston).

'Tudor' Window in the School Entrance Hall (see Appendix II)
(photograph courtesy of ABC Videos, Preston).

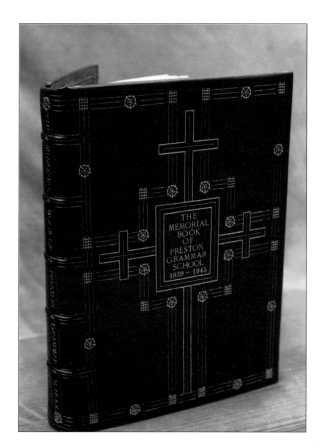

Left: Cover of 1939–45 War Memorial Book in Preston Parish Church (photograph courtesy of C. Williams). Below: Foreword to the Memorial Book by N. Hodgson (photograph courtesy of C. Williams).

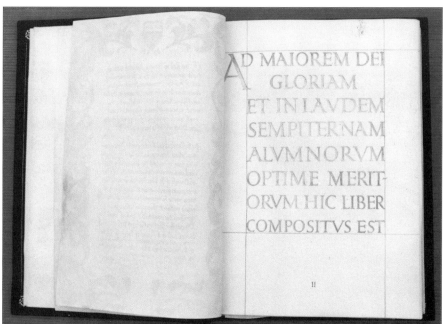

AD MAIOREM DEI GLORIAM ET IN LAVDEM SEMPITERNAM ALVMNORVM OPTIME MERITORVM HIC LIBER COMPOSITVS EST

11

School and House colours: Metal cap badge c. 1920–46; School Camping Badge; pre-1946 School blazer badge; post-1946 School blazer badge; Association colours (photograph courtesy Preston Grammar School Association).

Left: Preston Grammar School Association – President's Badge of Office (photograph courtesy of C. Williams).

Right: 1939–45 War Memorial Book – Arms (photograph courtesy of C. Williams).

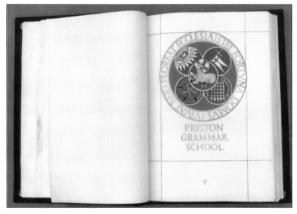

and that the Harris Institute should be asked to postpone the proposal to create a new school for the time being. Advertisements were issued, and on 19 May 1898 Frederick A. Hilliard MA of Merton College Oxford (BA London) was appointed Headmaster. He withdrew his application on 25 May, and the Rev. Henry Cribb Brooks MA of Trinity College, Dublin, and BA of St Catherine's College, Cambridge was appointed. It was a very good choice, and the School was saved.

Chapter 10

H. C. Brooks, 1898–1911

BROOKS WAS BORN IN 1857, and so was 41 at the time of his appointment. He did not go to Cambridge until 1893, and got his first degree there in 1896 (MA Cambridge 1902).

He at once made his presence felt by writing a letter to all parents of boys at the school in June 1898.

A letter to him from H. Hamer, the Town Clerk, on 7 September 1898, is indicative of the state of affairs. Brooks had asked the Town Clerk for the School records, and the Town Clerk replied that Beaven had not left any.

It seems that the School may have closed for a short time, because it is recorded that it re-opened in September 1898. The effect of the new regime is indicated by the number of scholars:

July	1898	44
15 February	1899	71
16 October	1899	109
	1900	114
	1902	146
18 June	1902	156

On 21 September 1898 Brooks submitted his first report to the Committee. He said that he did not intend to change the curriculum, and that in his opinion the purpose of the School was to prepare boys for the Universities in Classics and Mathematics. He had reorganised the School into forms, and considered that there should be graduated tuition fees, but no charges for extras. He had repaired the furniture, but there was a need for mats and decent washing accommodation. He had started a Physics laboratory, but the boys would continue to use the Harris Institute Chemistry laboratory for the time being.

In November the Committee authorised the expenditure of £740 on repairs, and in December approved expenditure of £225 on new lavatories and heating apparatus, and alterations to the WCs. Brooks reported that he had re-introduced Drill, and that the fees would be reduced from the beginning of the next term.

In May 1899 Brooks arranged for the Parks and Baths Committee to provide free swimming for the boys at the Public Baths from 12 to 1 on Mondays, and also for them to be able to purchase season tickets for 2s. 6d.

He prepared a brochure containing a short history of the School, and introduced the Founder's Prayer, which continued to be used (see Appendix V). He also gave attention to scholarships – 3 leaving scholarships from Thornley's bequest, and a scholarship of £30 per annum from the Goodair bequest were introduced.

In May 1900 plans for proper Physics and Chemistry laboratories were approved, to cost £400. The number of boys continued to grow, and by the end of 1900 reached 132, a figure that had not been reached for 17 years. As a result of this increase there were now 5 full-time and 3 part-time Assistant Masters. The number of changes and improvements that Brooks achieved in his first few years are clearly phenomenal. He rescued the School from its most serious decline, and ensured that it would continue to prosper in the future.

In September 1901 a prospectus was published. The subjects offered were: Reading, Writing, Arithmetic, Mathematics, Geography, History, Grammar, Composition, Literature, Latin, Greek, French, Natural Science, Drawing. Vocal Music, Shorthand, Drill and Swimming. Hours were from 9 to 12, and from 2 to 4.15, and on half holidays from 9 to 12.30. There was an extra half-hour per session for boys behind with their work. Homework was to last 1½ hours for juniors, and 2 hours for seniors. There were facilities for games and athletics. Fees were £2 5s. 0d. per term for boys aged 8 to 10, £3 0s. 0d. for those aged 11 to 12, and £3 10s. 0d. for those over 12. Younger brothers of those attending were to pay £2 0s. 0d., £2 5s. 0d., and £3 0s. 0d. respectively. There was an extra charge of 2s. 6d. for games. Sons of Guild Burgesses paid 2 guineas per annum, and there were a number of free scholarships, but even the holders of these, and the sons of Guild Burgesses had to pay 5s. 0d. per term for stationery, and drawing materials. There was a boarding house under an experienced Master, but no boarding fees are given. The fact that school caps were to be worn is stressed.

In 1902 the Council resolved that the Headmaster and boys should, in accordance with tradition, be invited to take part in the Guild ceremonies. As usual the Headmaster, and the Head Scholar were to give orations in Latin. Brooks issued instructions as to dress for those joining the Guild procession. All were to wear black coats, and preferably black waistcoats. Black ties were to be worn with broad (i.e. 'Eton' collars), but boys over 15 could wear 'inside' collars. The sixth form boys were to wear gowns and college caps with black tassels. All others were to wear school caps, scholars to have a black tassel, all others a blue tassel, and scholarship boys were to have their cap buttons covered in red. Monitors were to wear a blue rosette on the left breast. After the event the Committee placed on record its satisfaction at the conduct and appearance of the boys.

In 1904 the Committee agreed to admit 16 pupils who were preparing to take the course for pupil teachers – 6 guineas per annum was to be paid for each of them.

The law of secondary education had been changing. On 21 May 1900 the Town Clerk reported upon future national proposals for secondary and technical education, and in 1904 the Committee recommended the Council to take over the management of the School, and the Council agreed. Application was accordingly made to the Board of Education for the School to be recognised under the Secondary School Regulations. This meant that the Council would receive grant for the running of the School, but that the School would be subject to the control of the Board. The effect of this decision was momentous since it placed the School in the same position as all other secondary schools. If it had been an Educational Charitable Trust like so many grammar schools it could have remained a separate body, and might still have kept its identity, but the history of the School showed that it had lost any separate charitable identity that it might originally have had, and could therefore be dealt with by the Council at will. This was confirmed by the Board of Education in July 1909 when it was made clear that the School must be treated as a 'school provided by the Local Education Authority', and no scheme could be made under the Endowed Schools Act, or under the Charitable Trusts Act, and it must therefore have an Instrument of Government. This was a disadvantage in some ways, but there was a great advantage in the fact that the School now came under the control of the Board, because this meant that a high standard of accommodation and teaching would be insisted upon.

On 28 July 1904 the Council resolved to undertake financial responsibility for the School, paying the Headmaster, and all other Masters, and bearing all costs. Brooks' conditions of employment were to be varied accordingly.

The Council passed the resolution implementing these new arrangements on 25 August 1904. The Grammar School Committee, after consultation with the Headmaster, was to prescribe the general subjects of instruction, the relative prominence and value to be assigned to each group of subjects, the arrangement of School Terms, Vacations and Holidays, the payment of School Fees, the number of Assistant Masters to be employed, and their salaries, and, after like consultation, to exercise the power of selecting, appointing and dismissing Assistant Masters.

The Headmaster was to be responsible for the choice of books, methods of teaching, arrangement of classes and School Hours, and generally the internal organisation, management and discipline of the School. At the beginning of each term he was to submit a table showing the curriculum and the number of hours allotted to each subject in each form.

Brooks objected strongly to these proposals, and on 20 August 1904 he published an open letter to the Town Clerk in a local newspaper. He maintained that the Council's new policy reduced his position as Headmaster. Nevertheless the change was made, and Brooks received a salary of £400–£450 per annum. On 23 February 1905 the Council gave him power to appoint and dismiss all Assistant Masters (subject to the approval of the Committee) which may have mollified him somewhat.

In April 1905 the Board of Education informed the Committee that the School had been placed on the list of secondary schools, and that the position and duties of the Headmaster must be put in writing, and submitted for approval.

In November the powers of the Board began to be put into force, and the Committee was informed that partitions were necessary in the two large rooms, and that an Art room should be provided. The Committee agreed, and approved expenditure of work costing £950, but nothing was done for the time being.

In December Brooks reported that one third of the boys came from outside Preston, and suggested that the County Council be approached for a contribution to their education. The County Council responded by agreeing to pay a capitation fee of £2 for each boy from its area.

In June 1906 a letter was received from a Mr McNaughton, one of His Majesty's Inspectors of Schools. He had examined the School carefully, and was of the opinion that it was inadequate for its purpose, and could not be made adequate at a reasonable expense. He therefore considered that a new building was necessary. The Committee was not convinced of the need for a new building, and pointed out that an Art room and sanitary conveniences were soon to be provided. The Art room was to cost £700, and at the next Council meeting an attempt was made to have the question of its provision referred back to the Committee, but the attempt failed. The Inspector's formal report of 31 July stressed the lack of accommodation, and the necessity for a new building. In August another Government official intervened – the District Auditor, – who pointed out that the accounts of the School should now be incorporated in the Local Education Authority's accounts, and not kept separately. In November a letter from the Board referred to the Inspector's report, and complained that nothing had been done – in the meantime recognition of the School would be withdrawn. The Town Clerk replied saying that the partitions had been provided, and the Board accepted this for the time being.

In February 1907 McNaughton returned to the attack and pointed out that there had been a suggestion to provide a 'Higher Elementary School', but this would not be necessary if a new Grammar School was built, and he asked if work had begun at the School – it had not. The Board wrote again in May and said that patching up the old School would be mistaken and wasteful. The answer was a new School, but if this was not to be built the extensions must begin at once.

In July the Board took up another matter – it was necessary for at least 25% of the places at the School to be free places, and this figure had not been reached. The Committee agreed that 10 new free places would be provided.

In December the Committee stuck to its guns, and decided to continue with the proposed Art room, and also a Manual Instruction room, but on 29 January 1908 better counsels prevailed, and it was finally agreed in principle that a new school should be built, and a Sub-Committee was appointed to find a suitable site. The Board of Education thereupon agreed to recognise the School for grant purposes for the year 1906/7, and for 1907/8, subject to no time being lost in erecting a new building.

When Mr G. W. Martin retired from the position of Senior French Master in 1943 he gave a description of the Cross Street School as it was when he joined the staff there in September 1907. He was form master of L3 which he took for all subjects except singing and handwriting. There were three classes in the hall, which made work difficult. There was no Common Room for the staff, but there was an underground playground for the boys which was very useful on wet days. At the end of the hall was the stationery room where the Headmaster personally inspected old exercise books before handing out new ones, and where, incidentally, he kept his cane. Saturday morning was a school session, and homework was given for six nights a week. Ultimately, he said, the School was condemned by H. M. Inspectors as unfit for modern needs.

It took the Sub-Committee a year to find an acceptable site. At first the members visited some newly built schools in the London area to get ideas, and in July 1907 selected 10 acres at the North end of Moor Park. This did not find favour, and a site in Frenchwood was suggested. This was agreed upon in October. It was a piece of land bounded on the North-west side by Bank Parade Grounds, on the North-east by Oxford Street, and on the South-west by the River Ribble, and Avenham Park. The Board of Education at once objected strongly to the chosen site – it was considered to be not conveniently accessible for the majority of students, too large, at the bottom of a slope and too low on the river frontage. A site to the North of the town was considered more suitable. However the Committee made no further suggestions, and in March 1909 actually appointed Mr Woolfall of Woolfall and Eccles, Architects to inspect the Cross Street buildings, and prepare a report, plans and estimates for necessary alterations. His report must have shown the impossibility of providing an adequate school in this way, because in April the Committee finally decided to recommend a site bounded by St Thomas's Road, Moor Park Avenue,

Deepdale Road, and St Paul's Road. The Estates Committee was willing to let the Grammar School Committee have this land at a ground rent of 2*d*. per square yard.

On 20 July 1909 it was decided to adopt this site, and to build a new school with capacity for 250 boys (50 being under the age of 10), at a cost not exceeding £12,000.

An architectural competition for the design of the new school was held, and Conditions, Invitation and Particulars were issued. An Assessor for the competition was appointed at a cost of 50 guineas plus expenses.

The building was to house 250 boys but must be capable of being extended by 2 or more classrooms. There were to be 7 classrooms, 2 to accommodate 30 boys, and 5 to accommodate 25, a common room to house 12 masters, a dining room for 50 boys, and a playroom in the basement. It was to be built of 'Accrington', or similar brick, and must not cost more than £12,000. Designs were to be submitted by 1 October 1909.

A design by Messrs Woolfall and Eccles was selected in February 1910, and was approved by the Board of Education in September. Tenders were invited, and a joint Committee of the Education and Grammar School Committees decided to accept the tender of T. Croft and Sons Ltd to erect the school for the sum of £13,655. Consent to borrow the sum of £16,655 was to be applied for to the Board of Education.

When this resolution came to a meeting of the Council for confirmation on 27 December 1910, it was moved that the resolution be referred back for further consideration, but the motion was lost by 15 votes to 21, and the decision of the Committee was approved.

At the next meeting of the Council on 26 January 1911 the Town Clerk read a letter from the Preston Property Owners and Ratepayers Association dated 19 January 1911 stating that a public meeting had been held on 12 January, and had passed a resolution to the effect that it was not desirable to proceed with the erection of the building. Members of the Council had submitted a Notice of Motion to rescind the resolution of 27 December, and to refer the matter back for reconsideration of the whole question. this motion was lost by 13 votes to 29. Consideration of the application for borrowing powers took time, and in May 1911 a letter was received from the Local Government Board suggesting that the cost could be reduced by £357, and this was agreed to. Why there should have been delay to produce such a ridiculously small reduction is not apparent. In August 1911 it was decided that Councillor Cartmell, Chairman of both the Education and the Grammar School Committees should lay the Foundation Stone.

In the meantime there had been an inspection of the School in February 1909 when there were 155 pupils, of whom 62 had scholarships. The

'Class in Life' of the fathers of the pupils was analysed, giving the following results:

Professional or Independent	29
Merchants and Manufacturing	30
Retail	34
Farmers	7
Commercial Managers etc.	29
Service, Postmen, Artisans	26

92 boys lived in Preston, 62 in Lancashire, and 1 elsewhere.

It was noted that only 3 boys were taking Greek, and it was considered that the Head Master's salary was too low. (He was receiving £450 per annum.)

As mentioned above, the School now required an Instrument of Government, and a draft was approved in February 1911. This was confirmed in due course, and the Grammar School Committee became a Board of Governors.

While the building of the new school was in progress Brooks was appointed High Master of Manchester Grammar School, and submitted a letter of resignation on 18 May 1911 and left Preston on 27 July. He later became Vicar of Selside near Kendal, and died there in January 1935 at the age of 78.

Brooks was replaced by the Rev. Francis Ernest Brown MA, DD, of Hertford College, Oxford. He was appointed on 10 July 1911, but he resigned on 29 September, and left in December of the same year to become Headmaster of the Church of England Grammar School at Geelong near Melbourne in Victoria, Australia. He was important to the School, despite his short time there, in that he introduced the House system – four houses named after benefactors of the School – Goodair, Harris, Miller and Thornley. He was also very impressed by the gowns worn by the sixth form, and introduced gowns for senior boys at Geelong. In 1920 he returned to England on leave, and was invited to present the prizes at the annual Prize Giving. He wrote to the School in 1930 to say that he had retired, and returned to England. The Australian School had been moved to Cario, but gowns were still being worn. It is interesting to note that his successor at Geelong was Sir James Darling who established a branch of the school in the Bush at Timbertop, which was attended by the Prince of Wales in 1966.

On 26 October 1911 the Rev. Norman Trewby MA of Hertford College, Oxford was appointed Headmaster, and he took up office in 1912. He was to be in charge of the move to the new building, and to see the School through the Great War.

Chapter 11

N. Trewby, 1912–1926

HAPPILY the new School was not built of the hard red 'Accrington' brick (as had been the Park School for Girls some time earlier), but of a pleasant 'rustic facing brick', embellished with stone. At least one alteration had been made in the original design, for A. J. Berry, the Director of Education, in his book *The Story of Preston*, which he had written for children in 1912, included a picture of the School, then under construction, which showed, on top of the western tower, instead of the octagonal feature, a large clock surmounted by a pointed roof. It was also found necessary to re-arrange the outbuildings because of foundation problems.

One of the features of the Hall was an organ built by Henry Ainscough of Preston. This had been presented by Dr R. C. Brown, an Old Boy, and famous Preston doctor (he was later knighted). He was born at 27 Winckley Square on 2 October 1836, and attended the School from 1845 to 1853. He was a keen organist, and had presented organs to the Royal Infirmary (where he played every Sunday for the benefit of the patients), the Harris Orphanage and the Homes for the Blind. One peculiarity of the organ in later years was that the blowing mechanism was driven by a motor worked by Direct Current. As this was not available from the town supply the motor was supplied by a Direct Current generator which was, in its turn, driven by an Alternating Current motor driven from the mains! All had to be started up before the organ could be played.

A stained glass window of three lights, from Cross Street, was placed in the corridor outside the Headmaster's study. This has given rise to much comment and speculation (see Appendix VI). Other objects brought from the old school, were some ancient oak desks, heavily carved by previous scholars, the set of painted boards giving the names of holders of scholarships and exhibitions, and some oak panelling.

The Hall was decorated by 5 large historical pictures copied by a Mr Sommerscales from the originals in the House of Commons by Byam Shaw. These were presented by the Harris Free Library Committee, and showed the (mythical) Rose Garden scene said to have given rise to the symbols used in the Wars of the Roses; Henry VII giving a charter to the Cabots; Erasmus and More; the entry of Mary I into London in 1553; and Latimer preaching before Edward VI.

The building was officially opened by the Earl of Derby on Saturday 19

April 1913. The Boys and Masters assembled in the Old School Hall in Cross Street, and after singing the hymn 'Now Thank We All Our God', they walked in procession to the new School and awaited the arrival of Lord Derby, and the Mayor.

After the ceremonial opening of the main door all proceeded to the Hall, where a service was held, the singing being accompanied by an orchestra formed mainly of Old Boys. Speeches followed, including the obligatory Latin oration by the Captain of the School. Lord Derby made a speech in which he admitted that he did not understand Latin, and he was followed by the Headmaster, who gave his annual report. The building was intended to house 250 boys, and the actual number on that day was 172.

The Cross Street building was offered for letting, and on 17 November 1913 the Council resolved to let it to the Post Office Engineering Department for 7, 14 or 21 years at a yearly rental of £230. It was decided to spend £650 on the building to put it into a proper state for letting, but the actual cost of doing this was £750. In 1945 a letter appeared in the Lancashire Daily Post suggesting that the building should be turned into a community centre, as a war memorial, but nothing came of this as the Post Office was still in occupation. The Council decided in 1951 that when the lease came to an end in 1953 the building should be used for further education. In 1955, however, it was decided that the building must be demolished, and this was done in 1956. The Chairman of the Town Planning and Development Committee said that, though the building might have a certain amount of historical value, it was in a very bad condition internally, and could be classed as dangerous. It is a great pity that such an interesting building was allowed to get into such a state, and today its demolition would be looked upon as an act of Municipal vandalism – the saving of 'Arkwright House' indicates what can and should be done in such cases.

Some changes were made – a school clerk was appointed at a wage of £1 per week; a caretaker, and his wife were appointed to take charge of the building (he had also acted as caretaker at Cross Street), and 4 cleaners were engaged; a telephone was installed; an Assistant Mistress was appointed to take charge of the younger boys; and the Headmaster was permitted to take not more than 10 boarders. To house them he took Moor Park Villa.

Fees were fixed at £2 5s. 0d. per term for those aged between 8 and 10, £3 0s. 0d. for those between 11 and 12, and £3 10s. 0d. for those over 12, with the usual deductions for younger brothers. Sons of Guild Burgesses were to pay £2 1s. 0d. per year or 19s. 0d. per term.

From this time more information as to the day to day happenings in the School is available because December 1913 saw the publication of the School Magazine the *Hoghtonian* – which continued to be published, generally three times, but occasionally only twice, a year until July 1967.

When the Great War broke out two members of the School were on the continent, and had remarkable experiences.

A. C. Sinclair was apparently eighteen, and had set out to visit Germany on 24 July 1914. He stayed with a German friend in Celle, near Hanover. A week later war was declared between Germany and Russia, and he saw the mobilisation of the army taking place, When Great Britain declared war on Germany on 4 August (he states that it was 5 August), his friend decided to enlist, and his other friends were returning to school, so he thought it as well to return home, but he delayed trying to do so until 25 August. He then went to the military doctor in Celle, who certified that he was a schoolboy, unfit for service in the British Army. He then went to Hanover, and after some trouble, managed to obtain a passport. He travelled to Rotterdam by train, arriving there on 30 August., and then crossed the Channel to Tilbury. Today this story seems almost incredible – reminiscent of Sterne's *Sentimental Journey*, in which the author travelled to Paris, and was there for some time before he remembered that Britain was at war with France!

The other continental traveller had an even more exciting time. He was F. J. Jackson of Form Upper IIIa who set off on a bicycle tour of Belgium, with his father, on 23 July 1914. Approaching Luxembourg, they found that

Entrance of the School from Moor Park Avenue (scraper board, artist unknown). The original is the property of the Association and is deposited in the Lancashire Record Office.

the Germans had captured the town. They saw hundreds of German troops in motors, and fled in blinding rain, managing to get through a German checkpoint on the way. Arrived at Bastogne they took rooms, only to be told that the bridge was to be blown, and that they must cross it at once. They were unable to change any money, but managed to catch a train, and arrived at Ostend where they caught a boat for England.

It is amazing that two boys from the same school should have such adventures, and, to say the least, it shows a certain naivety. When a party from the School went to Germany at Easter 1938, it was with some trepidation, and that was sixteen months before the start of the Second World War.

Meanwhile the normal life of the School was disrupted. Masters began to leave to join the Forces. The first was McNicoll who joined the Seaforth Highlanders as a private (shortly commissioned), and Lawrence who joined the Royal Welch Fusiliers as a second lieutenant. In due course others left, and were replaced by temporary Masters, and later by Women Teachers. It was at this stage that Miss E. A. Furlong joined the School to be Mistress of the First Form, however she did not stay long as she left to become a nurse, and went to Serbia where she was decorated for her services before returning to the School at the end of the War. The changes in staff were very numerous, and must have affected the work of the School. When conscription was introduced the Committee backed applications for deferment by Assistant Masters.

Despite the War the Board of Education insisted that a Teacher be appointed for Manual Work (i.e. Woodwork and Metal Work). After some problems the School was recognised by the Con-Joint Board of the Royal College of Physicians, and the Royal College of Surgeons as a place of instruction for Physics and Chemistry. This no doubt benefited those seeking to study medicine. The School was also recognised as providing advanced courses in Mathematics and Science, which meant an increase in Government grant. Salaries of Teachers had to be increased, and the County Council had not increased its capitation grant, so in 1916 the charges for boys from outside Preston were increased by 13s. 4d. per term.

Many Old Boys joined the Services, and a Roll of Honour was established in the *Hoghtonian*. The Committee was informed regularly of honours granted to Old Boys, for example Lieutenant Cedric Naylor was awarded the D.S.O., and two bars.

Deepdale Council School was taken over by the Army, and became a military hospital. For a short time the Deepdale pupils attended the School for evening classes until they could be found places elsewhere.

The War did not reduce the numbers at the School. It had been built for 250, and by the end of 1914 there were already 217 pupils.

In 1915 a Training Corps was formed for boys over 14 to undergo military training. It was hoped that it would be officially recognised as an Officers Training Corps, but it does not seem that the application was successful.

The Roll of Honour continued to grow, and the casualties mounted, but the number of boys increased, and by 1917 had reached 240. By 1918 the figure of 250 had been passed, and had reached 270.

Christmas parcels were sent to the members of the staff who were in the Forces each containing a number of articles, including a pipe, but luckily someone remembered not to include a pipe in the parcel that went to Miss Furlong.

Forty-four Old Boys, and one Assistant Master were killed in the War, and it was decided to provide a Memorial. Money had to be collected and it was not until 1925 that the Memorial was completed. It consisted of a bronze tablet placed on the western wall of the Hall, with the names of those killed, and a magnificent stained glass window in the bay of the north wall.

The tablet and the window were both made by Barraclough and Sanders of Lancaster. The cost of the tablet was £150, and of the window £890 (including £40 for the protective wire screen). When the Rev. S. D. Smart, a long serving Assistant Master, retired on 10 September 1935 he presented wooden posts, and cords to be erected round the tablet.

The official description of the window in the *Hoghtonian* is as follows:

The Memorial Window, which occupies the great bay in the northern wall of the Hall, is an admirable example of the artistic possibilities allied to this beautiful craft. Unlike most War Memorials, the window contains little which would suggest to the casual observer the horrors of war, or the agony of the years which it commemorates. Only a simple inscription serves to show the purpose for which it was erected.

The central figure is Britannia writing in the Book of History the records of our rough island story. Round her are grouped a few of the greatest of the immortal characters who have helped to make that deathless story. Of kings there are Alfred the Great, founder of the British Navy; Edward the Confessor, whose Abbey at Westminster is the centre of our national life; and Oswald, King of Northumbria, illustrative of the strong Christian character.

Ranking with the kings are the immortals, Milton and Shakespeare, and the men of intellect, Bacon and Newton. Gordon is shown as representing the men who trod the paths of duty, and Wilberforce as typifying our national passion for freedom and justice. In the centre of the panel are the Arms of Preston, on the left of which is seen Dean Colet, one of the pioneers of education, and on the opposite side Helena of Hoghton, our pious foundress.

Round each panel is the foliated oak, symbolic of Britain, and the Royal Arms, surrounded by the Lancashire Rose, in the tracery above, together with the inscriptions 'Agincourt', 'Crecy', 'Trafalgar', and 'Waterloo', complete the scheme.

Below is the inscription, which is the key to the sentiments which inspire it – not the glorification of war, but just 'This royal throne of kings, this sceptr'd isle, this happy breed of men, this little world, this precious stone set in the silver sea, this blessed plot, this earth, this realm, this England.

There is no blatant patriotism, but that finer spirit of love of country of which Alfred Noyes sung: 'There is a song of England which none shall ever sing.'

This is an incomplete, and confused description – below the top band with the Royal Arms, the Lancashire Rose and the names of the famous battles are three bands each containing five panels. In the top band are Edward the Confessor, Alfred the Great, and Oswald of Northumbria, together with Shakespeare and Milton. In the centre of the next band is Britannia writing in the Book of History with a knight in plate armour on one side, and a soldier in Field Service uniform on the other. The other panels in this band show Francis Bacon and Isaac Newton. In the bottom band the Preston coat of arms is in the centre, and in the other panels are General Gordon, John Colet, Helen Hoghton and William Wilberforce. Underneath is the inscription 'This window was erected to the glory of God, and in memory of the pupils of this School who laid down their lives for King and Country in the Great War 1914–18. They gave their lives that we might live'.

Beautiful as it is the choice of some of those depicted in it is rather surprising. Edward the Confessor, and Oswald of Northumbria are odd representatives of English monarchs, Shakespeare and Milton properly represent literature, Bacon and Newton represent science, and Helen Hoghton clearly should be there, although she was not the foundress of the School which existed long before her days. John Colet was Dean of St Paul's, and founder of St Paul's School, and a worthy man, but probably he only appears because Trewby went to St Paul's School, and this seems an insufficient reason. Gordon is said to represent those that followed the paths of duty, but he had already been denigrated by Lytton Strachey in 'Eminent Victorians', and was well-known for not obeying orders. Wilberforce, although again a very worthy man seems a strange choice. Great battles are mentioned, but where is Henry V, Marlborough, Nelson or Wellington? Why is John of Gaunt's speech from *Richard II* cut down? Altogether it is of great interest and beauty, but puzzling.

On Thursday 11 June 1925 a short service of dedication was held. Councillor Snelham, the Chairman of the Governors, in inviting the Mayor to unveil the window, said that it was the most beautiful thing of its kind in Preston, and probably in Lancashire, and in this he did not exaggerate.

In 1919 Trewby issued the first of a series of prospectuses. The School is described as containing 8 classrooms, a sixth form room, Chemistry and Physics laboratories, a demonstration room, an Art room, a gymnasium, a carpenters shop, a boys common room, a dining hall and kitchen, and an entirely separate preparatory department. The fees were £3 10s. 0d. per term, and for younger brothers of boys already at the School £2 16s. 0d. per term. The School was organised as follows:

Junior School	Forms I and II
Main School	Lower III
	Upper IIIa, IIIb and IIIc
	Lower IVa and IVb
	Upper IVa and IVb
Upper School	V Form
	VI Classics, VI Mathematics and Science, and VI Modern.

Upper IIIb and IIIc were for scholarship boys, in Upper IVa and IVb there was a choice of Greek or Science, and the V form boys took the Oxford and Cambridge Joint Boards School Certificate.

In 1924 the fees were revised. Sons of Guild Burgesses were to pay 19s. 0d. per term, Preston Boys, not the sons of Guild Burgesses, were still to pay £3 10s. 0d., and if younger brothers £2 16s. 0d., but boys over 16 who had passed School Certificate were also to pay only £2 16s. 0d. Boys living outside Preston boundaries (unless the sons of Guild Burgesses, or Preston ratepayers) were to pay an extra £1 13s. 4d., but this would be refunded if the County Council paid a capitation grant. In fact the County Council had increased the capitation grant from £2 to £5 in February 1920.

In January 1920 a proper scale of salaries for Teachers was introduced. The Headmaster was to have £700–£750 (this was increased to £950 in March 1921); graduate Assistant Masters were to have £180 rising to £450 by 6 annual increments of £10 per year, and 14 annual increments of £15 per year, so that they had to wait for 20 years before reaching the maximum salary. Non-graduate Masters were to receive £130 to £350, rising by increments of £10, and non-graduate Mistresses £120 to £200, also rising by £10 increments. It must be remembered that the post-war 'boom' ended in 1922, and the Government Committee on Public Expenditure, chaired by Sir Eric Geddes, created and swung the 'Geddes Axe'. As a result the Teachers agreed to a reduction of 5% in their salaries. (The effect of the axe in elementary schools was to increase class sizes – over one quarter of classes had more than 60 children in them!)

In 1921 there were 32 free places, and the number was increased to 41 in 1924. Parents were now required to agree that their sons would remain at the School until the close of the School year during which they attained their 16th birthday, and had to sign a form to this effect in which they agreed to pay a penalty of £10 if the rule was not complied with. It was not complied with on many occasions and much of the time of the Governors was spent in deciding whether or not to enforce the rule.

At the Guild of 1922 the School was involved in the usual ceremonies, but on this occasion a pageant was organised, and the boys were invited to take part. Also in 1922 there was a further modern innovation when a wireless set was acquired, and in 1923 a gramophone and records were purchased to assist in language tuition, and for musical appreciation classes.

The Board of Education wrote in March 1923 stating that the School fees should not increase as boys grew older. The Governors disregarded this when fixing new fees in April 1923, but in July they received strict instructions from the Board, and the fees were fixed at 10 guineas per year, with a reduction to 8 guineas at the age of 16 if the boy in question had been at the School for 4 years. Boys in the preparatory department were to pay 8 guineas, the sons of Guild Burgesses £2 1s. 0d., and boys from the County £5 extra, unless a capitation fee was paid by the County Council. A further change was that the School was closed on Saturdays, and the Wednesday half-holiday was cancelled.

The School was now bursting at the seams, for in a building intended to house 250, by 1923 there were 343 boys. It was therefore decided that the School must be enlarged. Six new classrooms, and a new cloakroom were necessary, and the Borough Council instructed the Borough Surveyor to prepare plans and obtain tenders. The solution was to convert the cloakrooms into classrooms, and to provide a new cloakroom, 4 new classrooms, and a new Physics laboratory. A covered playground was also suggested, but does not seem to have been provided. The estimated cost was £7,600 later increased to £7,800, but it was not possible to go out to tender until January 1925, when the tender of Geo. Hill & Sons Ltd. was accepted in the sum of £8118 10s. 0d. Work started at once, but was not completed until 1927.

The *Hoghtonian* continued to be published, and in 1919 a short-lived publication for junior boys appeared called the *Lowforbian*. In the July 1925 issue of the *Hoghtonian* a section dealing with the Preston Grammar School Association appeared for the first time.

In 1925 Trewby announced his resignation on his being appointed Rector of Ripe in Sussex. He left in 1926, and died on 24 November 1938. He was replaced by Norman Hodgson MA.

Chapter 12

Norman Hodgson, 1926–1947

NORMAN HODGSON came from Westmorland, where his father had been Vicar of Nether Wasdale (with Wasdale Head). He was educated at Keswick School, and Queen's College, Oxford, where he was a Scholar, and obtained a double First in 'Greats'. He had served in France from 1914 to 1919, first as a private in the RAMC, and then as a Captain in the RASC, and was mentioned in dispatches.

His term of office began on 1 April 1926, but there was a gap between Trewby leaving, and Hodgson beginning, and during this period the Second Master P. G. Coles acted as Headmaster, for which he was paid an honorarium of 50 guineas.

Hodgson began by making changes. The School hours were altered. Hitherto they had been from 9 a. m. to noon, and from 2 p. m. to 4 p. m., but now they were to be from 9 a.m. to 12.20 p.m., and from 2.10 p.m. to 4.20 p.m. The Prefect system was reorganised and at once four prefects were chosen from each House, and a ceremony of appointment was held. (See Appendix V for the Prefects' Declaration.) The wearing of gowns by prefects was re-instituted, although this did not happen until 1928.

In 1927 the School joined the Save the Children Fund. Goodair and Harris Houses adopted a six year old Bulgarian girl called Irina Myrovitch, of Gallipoli, and Miller and Thornley Houses adopted a thirteen year old boy called Wilhelm Reindler of Vienna, and in due course letters were received from both children. Shepherd Street Mission was also the subject of financial assistance from the boys.

In September 1928 a report was presented to the Governors on the result of the School Certificate examinations. Fifteen boys took the Higher Certificate (equivalent to modern 'A' levels), and thirteen passed, one gaining a Distinction in Ancient History and Literature. Thirty-five took the School Certificate examination (equivalent to the modern General Certificate examination), and thirty-four passed, of whom twenty matriculated. Distinctions were obtained in sixteen subjects. This does not seem to have been a very good result, but in 1929 the results were rather better – eleven took the Higher Certificate and all passed, with one Distinction. Forty-nine took the School Certificate and forty-five passed, of whom twenty-nine matriculated, and there were thirty Distinctions. It is difficult to compare these results with the results obtained today at similar schools where it is not unusual for pupils to obtain nine 'A' passes at GCSE level, whereas when one boy obtained eight distinctions in the School Certificate during the 1930s it was considered a very exceptional result.

Despite the extensions more space was still necessary, and in 1928 the spare cloakroom was converted into a school library and form room.

In 1931 Hodgson suggested that a School Parliament should be formed. It was to consist of elected representatives from each form, chosen 'for their gifts of initiative and originality', the School Captain was to preside, and there were to be monthly meetings. Ordinary rules of debate were to be followed, anything could be discussed, and suggestions and criticisms of the government of the School could be made. As a result of this suggestion the Captain submitted a Constitution to the Headmaster. There was to be a First Chamber of elected delegates to meet monthly, and a Second Chamber of the prefects to draw up agendas for the First Chamber. There was also to be a Cabinet of three. The first meeting of the First Chamber took place on 28 January 1932. The first results were that three new societies were formed, the question of House Colours was considered, tennis was dismissed as 'a girl's game', detention was deplored as a punishment, and improvements were made in the School Library. Meetings continued, though not as frequently as had been intended, but in March 1934 the *Hoghtonian* reported that no meetings had been held that term. One meeting followed, but in the next school year there were no meetings at all, and the Parliament ceased to exist, which was unfortunate.

This is, perhaps the place to mention other extra curricula activities. The School Orchestra (founded by P. G. Coles in 1919) flourished, as did the Choir, under the direction of H. W. Norman. There were excellent dramatic productions, but all these activities were controlled by Masters. There were also numerous school societies covering all interests and hobbies and organised by the boys, but they were generally short lived. In 1932 W. H. Pulman, the Senior History Master formed a Boy Scouts Troop – the 50th Preston, which continued successfully for many years. Altogether the School was a hive of activity.

Hodgson was very keen on outdoor activities, particularly in his beloved Lake District. A School Camp was held at Dunsop Bridge at Whitsuntide 1928, but in 1929 a site was found at Rosthwaite in Borrowdale which provided a good centre for fell-walking expeditions. Camps were held at Rosthwaite until the site had to be closed in 1937, and in 1939 a new site was established in Wasdale, near to a cottage rented by Hodgson. Camps continued to be held there during the early years of the War.

Walking tours were also organised in Scotland, and abroad using 'Trike Carts', which were one wheeled carts propelled by hand. There were also extended trips to Belgium and Germany, using Youth Hostels, and day trips to places of interest such as London, York, and Stratford-upon-Avon.

In 1932 a new Science facility was provided when a Biology laboratory was built. The contractor was J. Turner, and the cost was £1,012.

Norman Hodgson MA, Headmaster 1926–47 (photograph courtesy of his daughters, Miss I. Hodgson and Mrs C. Millest).

For a number of years the Chairman of the Board of Governors had been Dr T. C. Derham. He was an Old Boy, and in November 1932 he became Mayor of Preston. At the Speech Day he described himself as 'a veritable Pooh Bah', being Mayor, Chairman of the Governors, and ex-President of the Association.

The organisation of the forms was changed from that of Trewby's day. Forms 1 and 2 remained as before. Lower 3c was for boys from Form 2, and newcomers who were fee-payers. Lower 3b consisted of boys with scholarships. The members of these two Forms passed into Upper 3b and Upper 3c respectively, and older new boys entered Upper 3a. At the Lower 4th stage there was some selection, for those not likely to succeed at School Certificate level at the first attempt entered Lower 4c, and the others were divided between Lower 4a and Lower 4b. In the Upper 4ths those in Upper 4a began Greek, or took extra French. They dropped Chemistry and Physics, and took Biology instead. Those in Upper 4c passed into Lower 5 where they took the School Certificate if thought desirable. Upper 4a boys entered 5a, and Upper 4b boys entered 5b where they had a choice of Latin, Geography or Art. The three 6th forms remained as before. Later, as the number of entrants increased, a new Lower 3a was added. By 1933 here were 53 free places per year, and the total number of boys was 450.

The fees charged at this time were £5 5s. 0d. per term for the Preparatory Department, £3 10s. 0d. for Preston boys, £2 16s. 0d. for younger brothers, and 19s. 0d. for sons of Guild Burgesses. Boys from the County paid £1 13s. 4d. extra, unless the County Council paid a capitation fee. Free places for Preston boys were subject to a 'means test'.

By the end of 1936 it was obvious that extra accommodation was necessary, and the Borough Surveyor was instructed to prepare plans for a new gymnasium and swimming bath to be built on the vacant land between the School buildings and Deepdale Road. In October 1938 the plans were approved by the Governors, but had to be withdrawn at the Borough Council meeting. It was then ascertained that the Board of Education would not consider new buildings, except in exceptional cases, but in May 1939 the Board was persuaded to approve a new gymnasium, but not a swimming bath. The coming of the war a few months later prevented any work being started.

The outbreak of war on 3 September 1939 had a much greater effect on the School than had the outbreak in August 1914. This was because of the fear of the likelihood of air raids. In fact there were no raids on Preston, and only a few bombs fell in the town. (This caused a number of the Burgesses to feel insulted because the Germans had failed to appreciate the importance of the town.) As there were no air raid shelters at the School it was decreed that the boys could not reassemble on 13 September, which had been appointed as the beginning of the new term. The members of staff were all available (except for F. P. Holden who was making his way home from Bucharest), and held meetings to decide what should be done. On 11 September assignments of work were sent out to the 450 boys, which were intended to last them for 2 weeks, and further assignments followed.

Old gateway transferred from Cross Street to Moor Park Avenue in 1932 (photograph courtesy of Lancashire Evening Post).

Arrangements were made for 6th form, and 5a and 5b boys to work in Masters' houses. On 18 September arrangements were made with the Park School to use some rooms in the Junior branch in Winckley Square during afternoons. It had been hoped to open the School on 2 October, but the shelters were not ready, and it was not until 9 October that classes were able to use the buildings – two classes at a time. Between 23 October and 6 November the Upper School attended during the first half of the week, and the Lower School during the latter half. The whole school assembled on 13 November, and thereafter attended normally, but the hours were changed to 9 a. m.–12.20 p. m. and 1.20 p. m.–3.30 p. m. This meant that few boys could get home for luncheon, and as the School catering services had hitherto only been required for those travelling a considerable distance, meat pies and tea were provided. Later, when the School Meals scheme began, more adequate catering facilities had to be made available.

For several years the annual Prize Day had been held in the Guild Hall, because the School Hall was too small. In November 1939 it was again held at the School, because Regulations banned the gathering together of more than 306 people in any building (except cinemas and theatres), and so the School Hall was large enough for the purpose. No outside speaker was invited, but the Mayor presided as usual, and the Mayoress presented the prizes.

In the April 1940 edition of the *Hoghtonian* the names of the first Old Boys killed in the war were announced – Gunner John Hodson and Flying Officer J. P. Trewby (son of the former Headmaster), both being killed in action. Details from Old Boys in the forces were included, and formed an important feature of the Association's section of the magazine for the rest of the war.

There were inevitable staff changes as younger Masters joined the Forces, and were replaced by temporary staff, both male and female, including the return of Miss Furlong, who had retired in 1937.

Many of the senior boys were members of Air Raid Precautions units, or the Home Guard. Fire-watching duties were introduced, and each night one Master and two boys were on duty at the School from 9.30 p.m. (7.30 p.m. in winter) until 7 a.m., for which they received 2s. 6d. per night (increased to 4s. 6d. later). Forestry camps, Farm camps and potato picking were also arranged, so that most boys had some part to play in the war effort.

Boys also joined No. 341 (Preston) Squadron of the Air Training Corps, and in 1942 a separate Flight attached to that Squadron was formed at the School. This was so successful that in 1944 an independent Squadron was formed – No. 2148 (3rd Preston) Squadron.

Very many Old Boys served in the Forces, and it is, perhaps, invidious to single out any for special mention, since so many served with distinction. I have, however, selected three as examples. Derrick Nabarro joined the R.A.F. shortly after leaving School, and became a Sergeant Pilot. In June 1941 he was shot down into the sea, near the coast of Germany, and was captured. In November 1941 he escaped and made his way to France where he was again captured, and interned in a fort in the South of France. In October 1942 he escaped from there and returned to England. He was awarded the Distinguished Conduct Medal – the first time this decoration had been awarded to a member of the R.A.F.

Two brothers, who both attended the School, were the sons of Major (QM) Norman Crawley, and both became regular soldiers. The elder, also Norman Crawley, on leaving the School went to Woolwich, and was commissioned into the Royal Artillery in 1937. He had the misfortune to be in Singapore at the time of the Japanese invasion, but managed to escape by boat, and after many adventures got to within 300 miles of Ceylon, when he was captured by the crew of a Japanese Tanker. He spent the rest of the war working on the Bangkok – Moulmein railway. After the war he served until 1962, retiring as a Lieutenant Colonel, having been awarded the MBE. He died in 1990. The younger brother, Douglas Crawley, went to Sandhurst, and was commissioned into the Loyal Regiment in 1939. He later joined the 2nd Battalion of the Parachute Regiment, and saw action in North Africa, Italy, and at Arnhem, where he was severely wounded and captured. He was awarded the MC and Bar, and later commanded the 1st Battalion of the Loyal Regiment. He retired in 1985, after 46 years service, and died the following year.

Of the Old Boys who served in the Forces, 68 did not return. It is interesting to compare this figure with the 45 deaths of the 1914–18 War, because in that war casualty figures were generally much higher. It must be remembered that there were far fewer Old Boys in 1914, because the School was much smaller, but the chief reason for the larger figure is that of the 68, 31 served in the Royal Air Force.

As a memorial a *Book of Remembrance* was prepared, giving the names of those who died. It was designed by Henry Ogle, a retired Art Master of the School (who had himself served with distinction in the Great War, and had been awarded the Military Cross). It contained 68 brief biographies written by Norman Hodgson, and arranged in alphabetical order in groups according to the service or unit, and each occupying one page. It was written and illuminated in gold and colour on sheets of the finest vellum, and was then bound in dark blue Levant Morocco leather with gold tooled lettering and decoration by R. L. Foreman, a Modern Languages Master of the School.

The dedicatory page reads 'Ad maiorum Dei gloriam et in laudem sempiternam alumnorum optime meritorum hic liber compositus est'. On the next page are the badges of the School, and on the following page are the words 'This book records the Names and Service of those Old Boys of Preston Grammar School who gave their lives for their Country in the World War of 1939–45'. The colophon reads 'This book, the conception of the Preston Grammar School Association, was designed and written out by me, Henry Ogle, in Cheltenham, and bound by Ronald L. Foreman. It was finished on the 1st day of November 1954'.

The Book was placed in an oak case in the School Hall in front of the bronze plaque commemorating the 1914–18 War. On Remembrance Sunday, 7 November 1954 a service was held in the School Hall, and was conducted by Rev. D. E. F. Ogden, an Old Boy. the Book was unveiled by W. G. Hunniball, the President of the Association. It is now in the Preston Parish Church (see Chapter 18), and contains the following additional inscription:

> This Roll of Honour, dedicated to the glorious memory of all those, the former scholars of Preston Grammar School, who laid down their lives for their country in the Second World War of 1939–45, and to the proud memory of Preston Grammar School itself, which served well the Borough of Preston from 1358 to 1969, is presented to The Right Worshipful the Mayor of the Borough of Preston by the President and Members of the Preston Grammar School Association this sixth day of May in the Year of our Lord One thousand nine hundred and seventy-three for deposit in the Parish Church of St John, Preston, aforesaid, there to remain forever open to inspection by all men nor to be removed therefrom to any other place without there first being formally signified the consent of each of them, the Mayor for the time being of the Borough of Preston, and of the Vicar of Preston for the time being, and of the President for the time being of the Preston Grammar School Association or their successors in title.

The inscription was signed by the Right Worshipful the Mayor of Preston, J. Dewhurst; R. G. D. Meredith, Vicar of Preston; A. T. Heap, Town Clerk; and John Brandwood, President of the Association.

After the War the School returned to normality, but at Midsummer 1947 Norman Hodgson retired on grounds of ill-health. On leaving he published a letter of farewell in the *Hoghtonian* – the following extract is most typical of him:

> If I am to be remembered at all, I shall prefer to be remembered rather for what I have tried to do at the morning service, or upon other occasions of assembly, than for any efforts in the classroom. From my position on the platform I have tried to put before you, as occasion offered, a certain conception of life and character, individual and communal.
>
> In so doing I have regarded myself as the interpreter for the time being

of what we call the tradition of the School.

I bequeath to my successor the continuance of this task. What kind of things Preston Grammar School boys learn at School is of considerable importance. *But of much greater importance is the kind of boys they here learn to be.*

I leave that simple thought with your readers as my last remark.

Norman Hodgson died on 21 February 1962.

Chapter 13

The last years, 1947–1969

THE NEW HEADMASTER was Eric Johnson MA, of Peterhouse College, Cambridge. He was appointed on 23 July 1947, but could not take up his appointment until Easter 1948. To cover the interregnum F. K. Dodson, the Second Master, was appointed Acting Headmaster.

There had been a great change in education as a result of the Education Act 1944 which provided that every child was entitled to free Secondary Education, which meant either at a grammar school, a modern school or a technical school, although there was no reference in the Act to the types of schools. The decision as to which type of school a child was entitled to attend involved selection at 11+, and so abolished the old system of a scholarship examination, and an entrance examination for those whose parents were going to pay fees. All Education Authorities were required to produce a Development Plan. The Preston Plan took a long time to prepare. It should have been issued in 1946, but the provisional draft was not available until June 1947.

In fact Preston did not have a good record in respect of Secondary Education, since it had the third highest percentage in the Country of children who completed their education in elementary schools – no less than 65%.

The proposals in the Development Plan in respect of the School, and the Park School were peculiar. It was suggested that the buildings should be vacated, and that the School, and the Winckley Square Annex of the Park School should be used for Further Education, and the Park School for Primary Education. To house those chosen for Grammar School education one new three-stream entry mixed-sex school was to be built, or, in conjunction with the County Education Authority, two three-stream entry single sex schools.

The assumption seemed to be that Preston alone only required one three-stream entry grammar school, despite the fact that there were already two 3 form entry grammar schools. Furthermore no attention was paid to the rapid increase in the number of children which, in due course, gave rise to the 'bulge'. It was already apparent that the School was only just adequate for the needs of the Town, because in 1947 the number selected for the School under the 11+ arrangements was 78 (i.e. a three form entry). The Plan was approved by the Borough Council, but there was strong opposition to the proposals concerning the grammar schools, and the result

F. K. Dodson MA,
Acting Headmaster,
1947–48 (photograph
courtesy of H. W. L.
Cumming).

was that in 1951 the Plan was amended to exclude mention of the grammar
schools, which remained as they were.

The number of pupils was increasing, and there were some minor
alterations to buildings, and the School yard, but it was obvious that an
extension was still necessary. In 1948 the vacant land between the School
and Deepdale Road was transferred to the Education Committee, and in
1949 plans for a new gymnasium and ancillary rooms at a cost of £16,500,
and for extensions to provide a new assembly hall at a cost of £20,000 were
approved. However no building took place, although increasing numbers
made it necessary for there to be a four form entry in 1953. An extra master
was appointed, and temporary accommodation was provided. By 1954 there
were 556 boys, whereas in 1948 there had been 480.

In 1955 H. Walters A.R.I.B.A. was appointed as architect to design
extensions, and Thomas Croft and Sons Ltd. carried out the building work

at a cost of £33,220. The extensions consisted of a new block of six classrooms with adjoining cloakroom and sanitary accommodation, and a General Science Laboratory. The work was finished by September 1957, but was not officially opened until 30 January 1958, when the Mayor, the Chairman of the Education Committee, and the Chairman of the Board of Governors all attended.

The new accommodation appears to have been adequate for the rest of the life of the School – in 1954 Johnson had estimated that numbers might increase to 650 or 700, and in 1956 he even spoke of a figure of 2,000, but, although 601 was reached for a short time, numbers soon fell back below 600.

During the 1950s it became the custom for the School to attend a special service each year at the Parish Church. These services took place at the end of the Summer Term.

In July 1957 Johnson left, and was replaced in September by Michael James Hugill MA, of King's College, Cambridge. He did not remain at the School long, leaving in 1961, and being replaced on 1 January 1962 by Bernard John Moody MA, of St John's College, Cambridge. During the period before Moody arrived Fred Pickup Holden MA, of Emmanuel College, Cambridge, the Second Master, acted as Headmaster.

During the whole of this period the School continued to flourish. In April 1961 it was the subject of an illustrated article in *Lancashire Life* which ended with the words – '. . . the school is going forward with a confidence, not only in itself, but in the future it plans to serve so well'.

Unfortunately this was not to be, as signs of drastic changes were already apparent. In 1959 the Government White Paper *Secondary Education for All* had been issued, and, perhaps as a sign of the times, from May 1960 there ceased to be a Board of Governors of the School, although 'visiting Governors' were appointed. All secondary schools in the Borough were placed under the control of two sub-committees – 'Designated Schools East', and 'Designated Schools West'. For some peculiar geographic reason the School was placed in the East, and the Park School in the West.

As long ago as 1914 an article had appeared in the *Association Magazine* which stated, 'The Grammar Schools of the provincial towns are doomed. Red tape and the varying conceptions of secondary education are doing their work, and woe betide the Grammar School which has not a sufficiently wealthy foundation to withstand successfully the assault made upon it by the provision of Corporation Secondary Schools – rate-aided and state-aided'.

These were prophetic words. As mentioned in Chapter 10, the ultimate fate of the School was decided when it was fully taken over by the Corporation, and became a Secondary School. Thereafter there was no chance of it becoming an Independent School, or a Direct Grant School.

The selection of children for grammar school education at 11+ was a matter which aroused difficulties throughout the Country. It was comparatively easy to select those who wanted a grammar school education, and who showed great ability, and also to identify those who did not want such an education, and were clearly not adapted for it, but there was a wide borderline of children between these two groups, and, particularly where there was a strong demand for grammar school education, it was considered unfair to 'condemn' a child to what was considered an inferior education. This was particularly so where selection was based, not on ability, but on the availability of places at grammar schools. One of the answers to this problem was to provide 'comprehensive' schools which would take children of all abilities, but by 1965 only 4.5% of maintained secondary schools were 'comprehensive'.

In January 1965 the Labour Government, elected in 1964, passed a House of Commons resolution noting with approval the efforts of local education authorities to reorganise on comprehensive lines, but adding that the method and timing should vary to meet local needs.

In April 1964 W. R. Tuson, the Director of Education, had produced a document called *Organisation of Secondary Education – A Reappraisal*. The Education Committee did not formally request it, and it seems to have been his own idea. It was revolutionary in its proposals, suggesting that instead of the eight secondary schools which provided a five year course, and the two grammar schools which provided a seven year course, there should be a number of comprehensive, mixed-sex, high schools providing a five year course, and a 6th form College providing a two year course. There would therefore be no 11+ tests, since all would go to the same type of school, and would pass on to the College if they wished to proceed to higher education. This involved the abolition of the School, and the Park School.

It is indicative of the attitude of Tuson (an old boy of the School), that there is no mention of the destruction of the 700 year old tradition of the School, or of any method of protecting it. It will also be noted that this report was ahead of its time, and before there was much evidence of the effect of comprehensive education, and very little evidence of the 6th form College concept, which necessarily abolished the prefectorial system which had great advantages in the keeping of order, and the prevention of bullying. The Government Circular number, 10/65, of July 1965 pointed out the disadvantages of such colleges.

There is no doubt that there had been, from time to time, a certain animosity towards the School in the town, and, therefore, among some of the Councillors. This is indicated by the campaign against the building in Moor Park, and the refusal to provide playing fields (see Chapter 16). Why this should have been is difficult to decide, unless it be the desire of some

1. Eric Johnson MA, Headmaster 1948–57 (courtesy of H. W. L. Cumming);
2. M. J. Hugill MA, Headmaster 1957–61 (photograph courtesy of Dr S. Coyle
of portrait by Edward Hall, in Whitgift School, Croydon, courtesy of the
School Governors);
3. F. P. Holden MA, Acting Headmaster 1961–62 and 1966–69
(photograph courtesy of H. W. L. Cumming);
4. B. J. Moody MA, FRTC, Headmaster, 1962–66
(photograph courtesy of Mrs Lynne Williams)

to achieve equality by the lowering of standards. Moody, a newcomer to the town, at the Association's Annual Dinners in both 1963 and 1964 said that he noticed an anti-School feeling in the town. On the other hand, Tuson said in his report that one reason for his proposals was the large number of parents trying to get their children into the grammar schools. The abolition of such schools was an odd way of satisfying these parental wishes. The School was generally open to all classes, and was never a 'middle class' school. In the eighteenth century, for example, it is said that the future Earl of Derby, and a gardener were school-fellows (see Chapter 17), and in the present century very many boys from poor working class homes gained scholarships. It was found necessary for the Masters to provide a fund from which sports clothing was provided for those who could not afford it. As mentioned in Chapter 10, in 1909, of the 155 pupils 26 had fathers who were 'Service, Postmen or Artisans'.

The new proposals were very strongly opposed by all those interested in the future of the School, led by Moody. Tuson issued a number of Memoranda varying his original reappraisal, but never altering the suggestions relating to the School.

In September 1964 a Parent/Teachers Association was formed. The obvious purpose was to protect the interests of the School, and this was attempted with vigour. A public meeting was held at the Public Hall, there was a press campaign, and a petition to the Council. In all this the P.T.A. acted with the Preston Grammar School Association, and the Park School P.T.A. As a result of this action, in March 1965 the Council decided to delay making any changes for a year, so that the national opinion on changes in education could be obtained, for it seems that the Preston proposals were unusual.

The P.T.A., having been formed, began a series of social, and fund raising events. There were trips to inspect Universities, dinner dances, visits to theatres, bring and buy sales, fairs etc. The result was that a considerable amount of money was raised, and used for the benefit of the School, even to providing armchairs for the Staff Room, and furniture for the Prefects Room. All this proved how beneficial it would have been for the School if a P.T.A. had come into existence much earlier.

In October 1966 the P.T.A. submitted a reasoned objection to the Tuson Plan. An alternative scheme had been prepared by the P.T.A. in conjunction with the Park School P.T.A., which, it was believed, would ensure that every child in Preston capable of following an academic type of education would have the advantage of doing so, and which would have preserved the two Grammar Schools. The receipt of the scheme was never even acknowledged, and clearly it was never considered.

Despite this, and other objections to the Tuson Plan it was resolved to go ahead with it, and in December 1966 the Council decided that children would not be selected at 11+ in 1967, subject to the Department of Education accepting the new Plan. The Department did approve the Plan in April 1967.

At the Municipal Elections in April 1967 the Conservative Party gained control of the Borough Council. This Party had consistently opposed the new Plan, and at the May Council meeting a motion was referred to the Education Committee stating that the approved Plan constituted an experiment to obtain comprehensive education 'on the cheap', and was in breach of undertakings that grammar school eduction would be preserved in the comprehensive system. The Education Committee considered the motion, but did not pass it, delaying consideration until December 1967. After further consideration the Plan was again approved in March 1968, and implementation followed. In the meantime, as there had been no 11+ selection in 1967, there had been a non-selective entry into the schools other than the grammar schools, and senior scholars had been transferred to the grammar schools' 6th forms.

It is said that Tuson was very proud of the fact that he had been able to persuade both political parties to accept his Plan.

Finance for the new 6th form College was applied for in the 1969/70 programme, and the Borough Engineer was instructed to prepare plans to alter the School for use as a 6th form College until the new one was built. There were, of course, further objections to all this, but they were made with no hope of success, and in September 1967 the School and the Park School were amalgamated.

Moody, having seen that the School could not be saved, left to go to Maidstone Grammar School in 1966. There was evidence of animosity between him and Tuson, for example the latter refused to attend a public meeting if Moody was to be there. It was deemed desirable for a joint statement to be issued to the Press 'to correct certain erroneous implications'. It stated 'Our relationships have always been and continue to be happy and are based on mutual respect for each other's professional ability and integrity. The Headmaster has not been in conflict with the Committee who have never had cause to question his professional competence and judgment over staff appointments or any other matter. The Headmaster's acceptance of another post is not related to any decision of the Local Education Authority concerning the appointment of Men and Women Teachers and the resignation is not related to "sinister activities" concerning the reorganisation of secondary education about which there is always room for honest differences of opinion and the best answer for which is now being sought in Preston in the full light of public discussion'.

Holden was appointed to replace Moody. He remained Headmaster to the end, but he had a long period of illness, and Warburton, the Second

Master acted in his absence. Notice of Intent to close the School was issued on 10 December 1968. Warburton reported on this to the Council of the Preston Grammar School Association in January 1969, and said that he could see no future for the School. There were no prefects, no societies, and the decline in discipline was in keeping with present tendencies. The 6th form College officially opened in the School, and Park School buildings in September 1969, the senior staff having been chosen in May 1969. Miss Shanks BA the Head Mistress of the Park School was appointed Principal with Holden as Vice Principal, a Senior Mistress from the Park School was appointed Second Mistress, and Warburton was appointed Second Master. In December 1970 Warburton was appointed Acting Second Principal. The pupils consisted of those selected for grammar school education before 1967, who were allowed to continue their education, and 463 6th form College students from other secondary schools.

There were long discussions as to the form that the new buildings for the College should take, and it was decided that it should be amalgamated with the Alston Day College and the non-advanced courses at the Harris College (which became Preston Polytechnic in 1974), to become a Tertiary College which would provide for all levels of ability in the 16 to 19 range. In September 1973, while building work was proceeding, Alan Davies from the Queen Elizabeth 6th form College at Darlington was appointed Principal of the Tertiary College. It was formed in September 1974, and the first phase of the new buildings was fully operational by January 1976. It was named the 'W. R. Tuson College', but the name was later changed to the 'Preston College'.

When the new College was opened the Brockholes High School was transferred to the School buildings, but the occupant is now called the Moor Park High School.

Thus a 700-year tradition of education was wantonly destroyed in the hope that a new and untried system would give better results. Whether this has been the effect I do not know, but the fact that other grammar schools still flourish is proof that the old system still had advantages.

As this book was going to press the Prime Minister, John Major, announced that he wished for there to be a grammar school in every town. Whether this will result in the present system being unscrambled remains to be seen.

Chapter 14

Arms, Mottos and Dress

I T DOES NOT SEEM that the School ever had a formal Grant of Arms. In late 1925 the Association contacted Portcullis Pursuivant at the College of Heralds (a most suitable person to approach in view of the prominence of a portcullis in the Arms). He appears to have been horrified at the Arms being used by the School, which he said were lacking in Heraldic arrangement. The matter arose because the Association was seeking a badge to wear on blazers. Some consideration was given to the possibility of obtaining a Grant of Arms, but it would have cost £75 to have the history of the Arms properly examined, and the Governors were not prepared to pay for it to be done. It was assumed that the Arms were of great antiquity, having been used time out of mind.

The Arms in question were those carved in stone over the main doors of the Cross Street School, and the Moor Park School. Whether they were on earlier buildings is not known. They consist of a rectangle in the centre of which is a shield bearing the Arms of Preston, namely the Paschal Lamb, couchant, bearing a cross with banner, and the letters PP, however in some copies the lamb wears a crown, and not a halo. As an addition to the Preston Arms, in the upper left corner of the shield is a compartment containing a hand holding a book, with the motto *Dignus es aperire*, which I take to mean *Thou art to reveal things of worth*. Behind the shield are a mace and a crozier in saltire. To the left of the shield is a crowned Tudor Rose, the badge of the House of Tudor, and to the right a crowned Portcullis, the badge of the Beauforts, from whom Henry VII was descended. On a ribbon is the motto *Vivat Rex Floreat Ecclesia stet Fortuna Domus*, i.e. *Long Live the King, may the Church flourish, and may Fortune rest upon this House*. On the Cross Street School 'Rex' was replaced by 'Regina', and the Association, after a debate, adhered to this on the somewhat specious argument that 'Regina' must have originated in the reign of some Queen who had shown special bounty to the School. There was no such Queen, and it seems clear that 'Regina' was used in 1841 in tribute to Queen Victoria. After her death the School reverted to 'Rex', but the Association did not, although on the cover of the *Outline History* published in the 1960s 'Rex' was used, when it should again have been 'Regina'. In this version the Arms were redrawn and the crowns were removed from the rose and portcullis.

A School uniform was never strictly imposed, except for headgear. In the nineteenth century boys wore college caps (mortar boards), which seem to have been unpopular. Towards the end of the century a modern school cap was introduced, but originally this had a tassel like the college cap, and scholarship boys wore a red button on top. The badge was a portcullis. In the 1920s a new cap was introduced which was black with a royal blue band, and a royal blue front segment. The badge was a metal shield with the Preston Arms in enamel. In 1932 a special cap for prefects was introduced, which was royal blue with a black front segment, and the same metal badge. In 1946 H. Ogle, the Arts Master, designed a new cap which was ¼ royal blue and ¼ black. The embroidered badge was again a portcullis, but with a rose over it, and the letters PGS. In 1954 a School brochure describes the uniform as being: cap, tie, blazer, and grey flannels, with a special jacket for the 6th form.

The tradition that senior boys wore gowns was of very long standing, and it is said that the custom dates back to James I's visit to Preston in 1617. There was a picture of this occasion in the Cross Street School, showing the boys wearing blue gowns, but the picture was only painted at the time that the school was built, and is no authority for gowns being worn in 1617. Whatever the truth of the matter gowns are recorded as being worn in 1880, and it was by no means a new thing. They were also being worn in 1911, when they so impressed F. E. Brown. At the opening of the new School in 1913 it is recorded that they provided 'a splash of colour'; and they were also being worn in 1919. The custom then seems to have lapsed, except for the Captain and Vice-Captain. (Could it be because the gowns were worn out, and no-one could afford to replace them?) Norman Hodgson was very keen to preserve old traditions, and in the autumn term of 1929 gowns were provided for all prefects. In 1937 the Mayor, Councillor J. Ward, commented on the condition of the gowns when prefects walked, as was customary, in the Mayoral procession on Mayor's Sunday, and contributed 10 guineas towards the purchase of a new set. Somehow this came to the notice of the Press, and the *Daily Mirror* published the following:

A KING GAVE THEM THIS PRIVILEGE

The 16 prefects of Preston Grammar School wear gowns, not only on ceremonial occasions, but at class, a privilege dating back to 1617. When James I visited Preston that year he said that the boys should wear gowns to add to their dignity. The custom lapsed until Norman Hodgson, Headmaster, looking through records found out about the old practice, and restored it. New gowns were needed recently. A well-wisher donated 10 guineas. The rest of the money was raised by social efforts at the school.

As in most newspaper reports there were a number of inaccuracies. Two

School Arms (redrawn and enhanced by Mrs Lynne Williams)

original gowns are now in the possession of the costume section of the Harris Museum.

The question of School colours is something of a mystery. The Association questioned a number of Old Boys who had attended the School in the middle of the nineteenth century, and ascertained that the School then had no colours at all. However about the turn of the century blue and white ribbon was used on cricket hats. At some time blue and black was adopted, but no-one seems to know when. The Association adopted blue and black with a narrow white stripe.

The House colours were: Goodair – Green; Harris – Red; Miller – originally White, but later Blue; Thornley – Yellow.

Until 1933 the School had no special flag, and the Cross of St George was flown from the flagpole. In that year an anonymous donor (the mother of a pupil), paid for a flag which was designed by H. Ogle. It was coloured blue and orange, and bore the Preston shield with the Paschal Lamb. It was dedicated on Empire Day (24th May) 1933.

Chapter 15

Scholarships and Prizes

IN THE MID-NINETEENTH CENTURY the School suffered from the lack of any scholarships or exhibitions providing assistance for scholars to proceed to a university. This situation was altered to a small degree in 1861 when John Goodair gave £200 towards a university exhibition. He was born in 1808, and was not, apparently, an old boy of the School. From poor beginnings he built up a large cotton business, and was a member of the Town Council. His gift was increased by his son, Colonel William Henry Goodair, in 1879, on his retirement from the mayoralty, by an addition of a further £200. The total amount of £400 was too small to finance an exhibition, and interest on it was therefore allowed to accumulate until it reached the sum of £1,000 on 31 March 1904.

In 1865 another exhibition was founded by Thomas Winckley.

A great cotton master in the town was Thomas Miller, of the Horrocks firm, who presented Miller Park to the Corporation. He died in 1865, and in 1867 the Miller Exhibition was established to provide £40 per annum, the money being paid by the Corporation out of his bequest.

Edmund Robert Harris, by his will dated 1 December 1876, created the Harris Trust which provided £100,000 for the Library and Museum, £100,000 for the Harris Orphanage, and £40,000 for the Harris Institute. As the son of the Rev. Robert Harris he also remembered the School, and gave £3,000 to the Corporation to establish scholarships. A scheme was approved by the Master of the Rolls on 19 July 1880 in an action called 'Jacson v. Queen Anne's Bounty' whereby two Harris Scholarships were to be established, one to provide £70 per annum for four years, and the other to provide a sum as near as possible to £70 for the same period (in 1883 it amounted to about £50). These scholarships were tenable at either Oxford or Cambridge.

Another benefactor was Edmund Thornley who by his will dated 28 April 1876, which was proved on 6 October 1878, left money to provide five Thornley Scholarships tenable at the school. Two of these were worth £7 10s. 0d. per annum, and the other three £5 10s. 0d. per annum.

In 1906 the Walton Scholarships were founded.

When, in 1911, the then Head Master, the Rev. F. E. Brown created the House system, the memory of four of the benefactors was perpetuated in the names of the four Houses – Goodair, Harris, Miller and Thornley.

In 1914 it was decided to merge the Thornley Scholarships with the university scholarships, as the provision of free places at the School made them unnecessary for boys attending the School. The result was that in 1914 one Thornley Scholarship was combined with the Miller Exhibition, in 1915 one Harris Scholarship was awarded, in 1916 the second Thornley Scholarship was combined with the Goodair Scholarship, and in 1917 the second Harris Scholarship was awarded. The cycle was then repeated.

In 1923 Lady Cartmell gave a prize for English Literature in memory of her husband, Sir Harry Cartmell, who had been Mayor during the War years, and Chairman of the Board of Governors. At about the same time the Rotary Club of Preston proposed giving a prize for a subject relating to Commerce, but I can find no further reference to it in later years.

There were still some Scholarships of £10 per annum for boys starting at the School, but, like the original Thornley Scholarships, they were no longer necessary. A Scheme was approved by the Board of Education to amalgamate them into a leaving scholarship of £50.

In 1931 under the Walton bequest two sums of £1,000 were made available to provide scholarships at Oxford or Cambridge, and in the same year the Elizabeth Poole Scholarship was founded. There followed the Albert Edward Cartmell Scholarship of £2,000 in 1939, the Hodgkinson Scholarship, also of £2,000 in 1940, the Mary Ellen Poole Scholarships in 1943, the Arthur Hodgkinson Scholarship of £2,000 in 1947 and the Fred Mayor Scholarship in 1952.

The Fred Mayor Scholarship was founded by his mother in his memory. He won a scholarship to the School when it was at Cross Street, and went on to University. During this period he was supported by his mother who worked in a cotton mill. He became Headmaster of Henry VI Grammar School at Hull, but died at the age of 54. His mother decided to perpetuate his memory by founding a scholarship. She lived in penury, saving all she could, and when she died at the age of 91 she was able to leave £2,500 to the School.

In his annual report in 1952 the Headmaster stated that the Scholarship Fund totalled £24,000, producing an income of £800 per year, and that the School was one of the best endowed Grammar Schools in the Country.

There were numerous book prizes – form prizes provided by the School, and others provided by donors.

An important cash prize was the Ascroft Prize of £10, which was awarded 'to the student who shall be considered the most meritorious student of each scholastic year, taking into consideration examination and/or Form work results and with due regard to such results, but coupled with consideration of the student's character and influence in the School and taking into consideration also (if thought proper) the athletic record of the student.'

This prize was established by William Fawell Ascroft in memory of his grandfather, who attended the School about 1814, and his father who attended in 1852.

The following is a list of the chief prizes awarded each year:

John Hunt Cup and Prize for Dramatic Recitation
Hamer Cup and Prize for Junior Dramatic Art
Rawlinson Cup and Prize for Mathematics
John Helme Memorial Prize
Hall Memorial Prize for Art
Sir Harry Cartmell Prize for English
John Foster Prize for Physics
The Mayor's Prize for Mathematics
Richard Durham Prize for Geography
James Harrison Prize for History
James Harrison Prize for Chemistry
1952 Guild Mayor's Prize for Biological Sciences
Sir John Myers Prize for Greek Testament
Sir John Myers Prize for Work Done Out of School
Warburton Prize for Modern Languages
Andrew Wallis Prize for Natural History
Walton Prize for Latin
Preston Grammar School Association Prize
Headmaster's Prize for Service to the School.

Altogether there was an adequate number of prizes available, but difficulties arose because the original grants were not always adequate to cover the rising cost of books, particularly after 1945.

Chapter 16

Sports

I T IS NOT POSSIBLE to say what sports or pastimes were popular with the scholars in early times. No doubt, like the boys of Eton College (according to Gray), they were wont

> To chase the rolling circle's speed,
> Or urge the flying ball.

They certainly seem to have played with hoops in the mid-nineteenth century according to the lithograph of the Cross Street School by Day and Son, which shows two boys so doing, and others playing leap-frog. Some form of football was also played in the School yard.

Cricket was widely played throughout the country in the nineteenth century, but football was not properly organised until the second half of the century.

The first attempt to introduce organised sport at the School was in April 1882, when a Sub-Committee of the Grammar School Committee was asked to find a suitable piece of land for a cricket pitch. There does not seem to have been much enthusiasm for this, because nothing was done, and in November the Sub-Committee was again asked to find a site. In March 1883 a Mr R. J. Flowerdew, who leased land from a Mr Strickland, offered to sub-let a field containing 4 acres 1 rood 21 perches of land for the playing of cricket. The rent was to be £21 per annum, the Corporation was to pay £5 towards the cost of drainage, and was to erect a fence. The right to graze sheep on the land was reserved. The Committee decided to defer consideration of the offer, and in the meantime asked if a portion of Moor Park could not be used. In April it was decided that Moor Park was too far from the School, and 'too public', and that Flowerdew's offer should be accepted. However it was not accepted, and in November 1885 the question was again asked as to why no cricket pitch has been provided. Again nothing was done until April 1886, when it was decided to provide a pitch, at a rent not exceeding £20. At the next Council meeting an attempt was made to defeat this proposal, but it failed.

Nevertheless at the next meeting of the Committee in May the resolution was rescinded, and the Ribble Committee was asked to provide land at the Holme which was in Penwortham, and had formerly been an island in the river opposite the end of Fishergate Lane. It was then pointed out that all the land at the Holme was let to a Mr Dodgson, but it transpired that he was willing to allow 10 acres to be used on payment of £15 per annum. This arrangement succeeded, and the agreement was renewed from time to time.

Association Football was played on a site at 'Riverside' also on the Penwortham side of the River, and an Eton style Fives court was provided at the School by Mr James Walmsley in 1900, so by that date the sporting facilities were reasonable, and programmes of the Cricket and Association Football Clubs were printed.

In April 1903 better accommodation for Cricket was found when the Preston Cricket Club agreed to allow the boys to play on its ground at West Cliff from 1 May to 31 July in each season at a rent of £30 per annum. Games could not be played on Saturdays when the Club First Team was playing, a separate changing room was provided, and strict instructions were given that the boys were never to enter the Club bar. The annual Athletic Sports Day was also held at West Cliff.

The move to Moor Park Avenue meant the abandonment of the facilities, at West Cliff and Riverbank, and the use of Moor Park itself. No area was exclusively granted to the School, and this meant the removal of goal posts after each match. It seems that the original intention was to provide an exclusive area, because at the Council Meeting on 27 February 1913 a minute of the Parks and Baths Committee said just this, but at the meeting the Chairman of the Committee asked leave to amend the resolution to provide that the Park Keeper should have power to let others use the pitches if they were not required by the School. This amendment was opposed, but was passed. On the 27 November 1913 a resolution was passed allowing £400 to be spent on levelling and draining the land allotted to the School, so it cannot have been of the best.

After the Great War it appears that serious problems arose. This may have been due to the fact that during the War the Park had been used for many war-time activities, and had not been properly restored. It is certain that the School was unable to play any Cricket in 1922 and 1923 because of the lack of pitches, and the annual Sports Day was held at Faringdon Park in 1923. In the same year a 'benefit' Cricket match was held at West Cliff between Preston Cricket Club and Lancashire County Cricket Club. This was attended by the School because the player to be benefitted was 'Lol' Cook who had been the Cricket Professional at Cross Street. There had obviously been a considerable decline from having a Cricket Professional to having no Cricket at all.

Football was still played, and in 1923 Saturday morning school was abolished, and Wednesday afternoon was set aside for games.

The School obviously needed a proper playing field, and in October 1920 the Governors passed a resolution to this effect, but there was strong opposition, and the request was refused by the Council. According to the *Preston Guardian* some Councillors had in mind that the School was intended for a particular class, and, until all classes could be treated alike, privileges should be granted to none! In April 1922 the Governors returned to the attack, and proposed that 9 acres of land at the North-east corner of Cromwell Road, and Watling Street Road should be purchased at a cost of £2,000. This resolution was again refused by the Council, but was again passed by the Governors in May, to no effect. In November 1923 the Governors placed £2,000 for playing fields in their estimates for the next financial year. Luckily the 'levelling down' attitude of some of the Councillors did not prevail for long, and in July 1924 land for the new playing fields was found at Walton.

It consisted of 22¼ acres providing 12 Football pitches, and a 75 yards square for Cricket. The layout plan was referred back by the Council in December 1924, but was finally approved. In April 1924 a groundsman had been appointed, and a grass-cutter, and roller were purchased. The land was a long way from the School, liable to flooding, and the changing facilities were, at first, non-existent. A wooden hut was provided in March 1927 at a cost of £140, and was described as a temporary pavilion, but it lasted for 8 years. No water was available, and there were no washing facilities until, in December 1931, it was decided to erect a roof over a few cold water taps and bowls at a cost of £250. the Headmaster had started to raise a fund to provide a proper pavilion, which he intended should reach £3,000. By December 1933 it had only reached £500, but the Governors then decided that a pavilion should be built at a cost of £1,150. The resolution had to be withdrawn at the Education Committee, but in July 1934 the Board of Education agreed that a pavilion could be built. In September the Board discovered that no provision was to be made for hot water, and insisted that hot water was necessary.

A contract was entered into with R. M. Barton and Sons to build the pavilion at a cost of £1,362 in December 1934, and it was ready for use in 1935.

From 1930 until his retirement in 1966 the playing fields were in the care of Ernest Adams (except for the war years when he served in the Army). Known to generations of boys as 'Ernie', he managed to keep the pitches in good condition, despite occasional difficulties when the River overflowed. On his retirement he was presented with a gold watch by the boys of the School.

The history of the provision of sporting facilities for the School obviously does not redound to the credit of the Borough Council. It took four years to find a Cricket ground, fifteen years to provide proper playing fields for the new School (and when found they had bad faults), and the playing fields were lacking in proper changing and washing facilities for ten years.

Despite these disadvantages the School achieved a notable record, both in Association Football, and Cricket, and in the athletic events which were held annually.

When E. Johnson became Headmaster in 1948 he introduced Rugby Football as an alternative to Association Football. This aroused some opposition, particularly from Old Boys, and it took some time for the School teams to become competitive (in its first match, which was against Hutton Grammar School, the First Team lost 18–0!) As mentioned above there was an annual athletic meeting, and regular cross-country runs.

As regards other sports, from time to time lawn tennis flourished. Swimming was introduced in 1900 when the Parks and Baths Committee of the Corporation granted the School exclusive use of the Saul Street Baths for 2 hours per week in May, June and July. This was not continued, no doubt because of the condition of the Baths. In 1936, when the new Baths were opened it was suggested that swimming should be renewed as a sport. In 1937 a swimming Cup was obtained, and some swimming and life-saving classes were held. When the ATC Squadron was formed the members engaged in competitive swimming, and this continued after the War. Hockey was played – occasionally against the Park School, and Badminton was played for a time. However these 'minor' sports never achieved the popularity of Football and Cricket.

The introduction of the House system in 1911 gave rise to keen inter-house rivalry, and this was encouraged by the presentation of trophies for inter-house sport, namely:

Anderson Cup for Association Football
Lucas Shield for the best athlete
Heald Cup for Cricket
Watt Cup for Cross-Country Running
Trewby Memorial Cup for Tennis
Old Boys' Cup for Association Football (six-a-side)
Old Boys' Cup for Rugby Football (seven-a-side)
Harrison Cup for Rugby Football
Rook Memorial Cup for Cross-Country Running
Sunderland Challenge Cup for Junior Athletics
Foster Challenge Cup for Athletics.

In addition Coronation Cups were purchased in 1937, from funds provided by the Borough Council, for Gymnastics, Boxing and Swimming, and in 1953 a House Championship Cup was similarly acquired.

Although hardly classed as a sport inter-House singing competitions were held each year, and a fine silver shield, designed by H. Ogle, was awarded to the winning House.

Chapter 17

Some Famous Old Boys

THROUGHOUT ITS HISTORY the School produced many men who rose to the top of their chosen professions or callings, and therefore became famous. Others were not so successful in a worldly sense, but have filled their places in Society in an honourable manner to the credit of the School. I have found difficulty in choosing those to be mentioned in this chapter, and I have, therefore, included only six, five of whom are long dead, and one who is still alive, but who must be one of the most unusual Old Boys.

Edward Stanley

The Stanley family has always had close connections with Preston, but only one member of the family is known to have attended the School. This was Edward Stanley who was born in Patten House, which was situated on the north side of Church Street, on 12 September 1752. He attended the School about 1760 when Henry was Headmaster, and completed his education at Trinity College, Oxford. In February 1776 his grandfather, the 11th Earl of Derby, died, and as his father was already dead, Edward succeeded as 12th Earl of Derby. He was a great sportsman, particularly interested in horse racing, and cock fighting. He is chiefly famous for founding the Derby, and the Oaks races.

John Danson is said to have been at the School at the same time as Stanley. He was Quaker, and a gardener by trade. He was a tenant of one of Stanley's cottages in Preston, and, falling on hard times was unable to pay his rent, and was threatened with eviction. He therefore walked to Knowsley Hall, and knocked on the front door. To the footman who answered he demanded to see 'Edward'. Being asked who Edward was he replied 'Edward Stanley'. By dint of steady perseverance he succeeded in seeing the Earl, and explained his difficulties. Because they had been at school together the Earl excused him his debt, and said that he could live rent free for the rest of his life. Some time later they met in Preston during Race Week. The Earl was going to a cock fight, and Danson said to him 'I see Edward thou hasn't given up thy silly sinful practices'. The Earl replied 'If all my tenants paid like you do I would have to!'. This is a delightful story, but Danson died in 1812 at the age of 73. He was therefore 13 years older than the Earl, and it is unlikely that they were at the School at the same time.

Edward Baines

The father of Edward Baines set up business as a grocer in Preston, but he was not a Guild Burgess, and so was not entitled to do so. The Corporation, possibly on political grounds, for he was a Whig, brought an action against him, and he was forced to move to Walton-le-Dale in 1770. Here Edward was born in 1774. He was sent to live with an uncle in Westmoreland, and, for a time, attended Hawkshead Grammar School, while Wordsworth was also a pupil there. He returned to his family when he was eight, and was sent to the School, and spent some years in the lower School. According to his *Life*, written by his son, only the sons of freemen could move to the higher School, but this is not true. The son adds that the Master – presumably the Usher – was pompous and ill-educated, and only taught writing and accounts, and scarcely the elements of Latin. He used to say 'I profess to be a practical school master, and to teach English, but not to be a "classic".'

During Baines's time at the School there was a 'barring-out' by the boys. The doors of the school were fastened with huge nails, but one of the younger boys was let out to get food for the rest. It lasted for two or three days. Then the Mayor, and officers were sent for to speak to the boys. Baines answered the magisterial summons by declaring that they would not give in unless assured of a full pardon, and a certain length of holidays. The Mayor gave them until evening to consider what they would do, but on his return he found the doors open. The boys had fled to Penwortham Woods, and returned to their homes after dark – no one was punished. Later Baines is alleged to have stolen the halberds from outside the Mayor's front door, and thrown them into a reservoir, and he also once fired a pistol over a lady's head, for which he spent a night in gaol.

Baines became a journalist, and for a number of years was MP for Leeds, but his chief claim to fame consists of the local history books that he wrote – his *History, Directory, and Gazetteer of the County Palatine of Lancaster* which he published in 1825, and his much larger *History of the County Palatine of Lancaster* published in 1836. He died in 1848.

Sir John Eldon Gorst

Born in Preston on 24 May 1835, he attended the School, and was Captain in 1852–53. In 1853 he went to St John's College, Cambridge, and was Third Wrangler in 1857, and a Fellow from 1857 to 1860. During part of this period he became a Master at Rossall College so as to be near his father, who was very ill.

In 1859 he sailed to New Zealand on a sailing ship, marrying on the way. He became involved in Maori affairs, and in 1861 became Inspector of Native and Missionary schools in Waikito. In 1862 he became Civil Commissioner in Waikito, and edited a newspaper, but in the Maori uprising he and his family had to flee for their lives. He returned to England, and was called to the Bar in 1865. In 1866 he became M.P. for Cambridge, and, at the request of Disraeli, reorganised the Conservative Party, and was thus mainly responsible for the election victory of 1874. In 1880 he became friendly with Lord Randolph Churchill, and worked with him in Parliament. He was Solicitor General in 1885, Under-Secretary of State for India in 1886, Financial Secretary to the Treasury in 1891, and Vice-President of the Committee of the Privy Council on Education (in effect Minister of Education), in 1895.

Owing to the Free Trade and Tariff Reform controversy he left the Conservative Party, and in 1910 stood as a Liberal candidate for Preston, but was not elected. He died on 4 April 1916.

Sir Percy Henry Noel Lake KCB

He was born in 1855, son of a Canadian officer, Lt-Col. P. G. B. Lake, who was serving in the British Army. He attended the School before going on to Uppingham. In 1873 he joined the 59th Foot (later 2nd Battalion East Lancashire Regiment). He served with distinction on the North-West Frontier of India, and in the Sudan. He became a Staff Officer, particularly concerned with intelligence, and also spent a considerable time in Canada organising the Militia. Promoted to Lieutenant-General in 1911, he was sent to India to command the Meerut Division, and in 1912 was appointed Chief of General Staff in India.

In 1915 the ill-advised attempt to advance on and capture Baghdad led to the British and Indian force under the command of Major-General Townsend being besieged in Kut-el-Amara. In 1916, after the failure to relieve Kut, Lake was sent to take command of the Tigris Force from Sir John Nixon, and a second attempt was made to relieve Kut, which again resulted in failure. The fall of Kut followed, and the death of nearly 6,000 men, either in the siege or on the death march of the prisoners after the surrender. Lake was preparing for a new campaign when he handed over command of the Army in Mesopotamia to Major-General F. S. Maude, and returned to England to give evidence to the Mesopotamia Committee. He was appointed KCB, and worked in the Ministry of Munitions. In 1919 he retired from the Army, and settled in Canada.

He had a brilliant army career, but was unfortunate in being, near the end of it, placed in command of a most difficult situation at the age of 61, having had little experience of command of a large army in action. General Maude testified to the excellent foundation work which he had put in and which led to the future success of the campaign.

He was a member of the Association, and was for many years a Vice-President. He died in 1940 at the age of 85.

Sir John Linton Myers OBE, MA, FSA

He was the son of the Rev. Miles Myers, Vicar of St Paul's Church, who had been Captain of the School. Born in 1869 he attended the School until he obtained a scholarship to Winchester, from where he went to New College, Oxford. He took first classes in Honours Moderations (1890), and Litterae Humaniores (1892). He then carried out archaeological work in the eastern Mediterranean, particularly in Crete, Cyprus and Egypt. He became University Lecturer in Classical Archaeology at Oxford, and then was appointed Professor of Greek at Liverpool. In 1910 he returned to Oxford as Wykeham Professor, and remained there until his retirement in 1939.

During the Great War Myers served as a Lieutenant-Commander in the Royal Navy. He was sent to the Aegean where his knowledge of Greek, and of the geography of the area were of great advantage in the intelligence work that he carried out. He collected a gang of Greek ruffians, and in the tug 'Syra' and later in the former Royal yacht 'Aulis' he led expeditions on to the west coast of Turkey, particularly engaging in cattle raids. He had a large black beard and Compton Mackenzie, with whom he worked, said that he looked like an Assyrian king, with a touch of Blackbeard Teach, the pirate.

He continued to take an interest in the School until his death in 1954, and for many years was a Vice-President of the Association. Miles Myers, his father, established a prize for Greek Testament, and this was added to by his son, who also founded a prize for work done out of school.

Mohamed Mahdi al-Tajir

Born in Bahrein in 1931, this distinguished Arab diplomat and business man attended the 6th form of the School in 1947 for several terms. In 1956, at the aged of 24 he became Director of Port and Custom Services in Bahrein. In 1963 he moved to Dubai as Director of H. H. the Ruler's Personal Affairs, and Petroleum Affairs. He became a director of the National Bank of Dubai, and of numerous financial and other companies. He was the Ambassador of the United Arab Emirates to the United Kingdom from 1972 to 1986, and to France from 1972 to 1977. He is an Honorary Citizen of the State of Texas USA, and is said to be one of the richest men in the world. He mentions his attendance at the School in his *Who's Who* entry.

Chapter 18

Preston Grammar School Association

A T VARIOUS TIMES during the latter part of the nineteenth century the Old Boys of the School organised social and recreational events. In particular a dinner was held at the Park Hotel on the 6 January 1888, when the chair was taken by John Addison QC, M.P.

There was an Old Boys football club, of which the Earl of Derby was President, between 1906 and 1908, but it is not known whether the Association then existed in any form.

In 1908 the Association was definitely formed, due chiefly to the work of Keith H. Moore. A constitution was prepared, and between 1910 and 1914 a magazine was published with Moore as editor.

Annual dinners were held – the menu for that of 18 January 1911 was as follows: Oxtail and Tomato Soup; Silver Hake with Cockle Sauce; Fried Fillet of Whiting with Anchovy Sauce, Sirloin of Beef with Horseradish Sauce; Boiled Mutton with Caper Sauce; Roast Gosling with Apple Sauce Jelly; Christmas Pudding with Rum Sauce; Mince Pies; Jellies; Blancmange; Cheese; and Salad – they ate rather well in those days.

It was decided to hold a competition for a School Song, with a prize of one guinea, but only one entry was received. It was to be sung to the tune of the 'Soldiers Chorus' from Gounod's 'Faust', and the chorus was:

> Sing then, and loudly, the glad refrain,
> Joyous to honour the School again,
> Ring then, and proudly, the loyal strain,
> Long may the School, and long may the School flourish and reign.

There were two verses – the author was not awarded the prize. Some years later, in 1914, but before the war broke out, another would-be poet produced a somewhat bellicose song to the tune of 'Forty Years On'. The chorus was:

> Sons of the School, rally together,
> Stand back to back, and fight with a will,
> Fight for the School through fair or foul weather,
> Give what she gave to you – courage, and skill.

Again no prize was awarded.

As there were no official School colours, royal blue and white were decided upon, and hat bands were ordered, presumably for the straw hats

of the period. The advisability of introducing Rugby Football to the School
was discussed, and the views of Headmasters of schools which played Rugby
were obtained, and were very favourable, but it was to be nearly forty years
before anything came of this. It is clear that then, as well as later, the
members were widespread, since in one issue of the magazine there were
letters from Singapore, Jamaica and (rather surprisingly) from the Kansas
City Cricket Club of Kansas City, Missouri.

The activities of the Association included dinners, smoking concerts, and
a ladies evening. It is also noteworthy that the orchestra which played at
the opening of the new School was composed largely of Old Boys.

By May 1914 there were 190 members, but when the Great War broke out
most of the active members joined the Forces, and the Association was
suspended.

Moore was killed in the war, and it was not until 1925 that the Association
was revived, chiefly due to the actions of two of the Masters – J. McNicoll
and F. K. Dodson. A meeting was held at the White Horse Restaurant in
that year, and, after some difficulties, the Assocation was reformed, and has
continued to this day.

It was decided to reform the Sections which had existed before 1915, and
the Athletic Section was formed in 1925, and a Debating Section in 1926.
An attempt to form a Dramatic Section failed for lack of support. 'Group
Sections' were set up to try and group together members who had been at
the School at the same time, but this system never worked very well.

The Athletic Section was very successful, and organised a number of
Football teams. Later swimming and rambling were added, and also golf,
which is now, alas, the only game that most members of the Association
can manage to play.

It was arranged with Trewby that the *Hoghtonian* would in future contain
an Association section, and that copies of the magazine would be supplied
to all members. The first issue to contain an Association section was published
in July 1925. At that time there were 135 members, and the President was
Sir Charles Brown.

It was considered that the Association should have a badge, and, after a
reference to the College of Heralds (see Chapter 14), a gold portcullis was
chosen. The colour of the tie was black and royal blue stripes, with a narrow
white stripe between, and blazers were made with the same stripes, and a
gold wire portcullis on the pocket. They were somewhat startling to behold,
and the cloth was referred to as the 'Butchers Apron' pattern. These blazers
cost £2 12s. 6d., but the badge could be bought for 7s. 6d., and sewn on
a plain blue blazer. By July 1927 there were 250 members, and it was
calculated that this amounted to one-fifth of those eligible to join.

In that year 60 members of the Athletic Section joined the Preston

Hospitals' fund raising 'Rag' which included a 'Chinese Invasion of Preston' (this was before the days of Chinese Restaurants), and a 'Chinese Execution' at the front of the Harris Museum which involved the beheading of a dummy. In fairness to the Athletic Section they had been unable to play Cricket because a ground could not be found.

Annual dinners were held, starting in 1926, and from 1932 to 1936 were held in the School Hall.

A London Section was formed, and, for a time held monthly luncheon meetings at the Column Club in Salisbury Square. On 14 February 1930 a double event was arranged when the Association held a dinner at the White Horse Restaurant, and the London Section held a dinner at the Criterion on the same evening. This was repeated in subsequent years.

From 1932 the School Sports Day was held on a Saturday, making it easier for Old Boys to attend. A special enclosure was provided for the Association, and there were events for Old Boys.

When War broke out in 1939 it was decided to keep the Association in being, and a 'Forces Register' was set up to keep contact with Old Boys in the Forces. This led, in due time, to the arrangements to provide the Memorial Book (see Chapter 12).

After the War a Cricket Section was established, and a Social Committee, but the Annual Dinner was not re-established until Guild Year 1952.

The 1947 Draft Development Plan of the Borough Council caused great concern when it was produced, and it was strongly resisted by the Association, but the Council refused to alter the Plan. This resulted in an appeal to the Minister of Education, which, after some time, resulted in the Plan being approved subject to the amendments relating to the School which the Association had recommended.

In the late 1940s the Association publicised the fact that boys living in the County area could still attend the School, which resulted in an improvement in the number of entries from the County.

The London Section was reformed in 1948, and still continues to hold meetings, drawing members from the South of England generally.

Annual Dinners have been held regularly, but at different locations – for a time at the Clifton Arms Hotel at Lytham, then at the Bull and Royal Hotel in Preston, until its closure, then at the Trafalgar Hotel at Samlesbury, and Broughton Park Hotel. For a number of years successful Dinner Dances were held, but support dwindled, and none were held after 1971.

The Athletic Section had always been organised somewhat separately from the rest of the Association. It generally had four football teams playing in the Lancashire Amateur Leagues, and, apart from occasional difficulties about pitches, was very successful. Finance proved to be a problem, as the cost of transport for the 'away' games increased. This was solved by holding four dances a year. Tickets for these were sold at the beginning of each year, and were always sold out. The result was an increase of revenue for the Association as a whole. Some of those who played for the Athletic Section were not members of the Association, and in 1953 it was resolved that all members of the Section must join the Association. A year later it was found that twenty members of the Section were still not members of the Association, but the Secretary of the Section promised that in future all would join. In fact this did not happen, and the matter was raised from time to time over the years. After the closure of the School the Section had difficulty in recruiting members, and players were accepted who, not only were not members of the Association, but had not attended the School. Ultimately, in 1977, it was decided to wind up the Section, as part of the Association, on 30 June 1980. To settle the financial position the Association paid to the Section £100 per year until that date. A new club was then established called 'Preston Grammar School Associates', and still continues to flourish.

In 1958 a Golf Section was formed, and an annual competition was instituted for a cup provided by the Association. Teams have also played in the Lancashire Old Boys' competition with some success.

In 1954 it was decided to have a new design for the Association Badge. The design chosen was a shield with a gold border. In the top part of the shield (the'chief'), there are three Tudor roses on a white ground, and in the bottom half (the 'base'), there is a gold portcullis on a blue ground. Beneath are the letters PGSA.

In the same year it was suggested that the Association might benefit by contact with other Old Boys' Associations. A Fylde Association had been formed, and delegates were sent to its meetings. No advantages seem to have resulted, and the Fylde Association was disbanded in 1959. In 1963 the Old Rochdalians' Association suggested the formation of a North West Old Boys' Association, but the Preston Association decided not to join.

There was a constant effort to recruit members, particularly from School leavers. In 1961 it was decided to award a prize of £7 15s. 0d. each year to a School leaver chosen by the Headmaster, but the boy was only to received £2 10s. 0d. in cash, the balance of £5 5s. 0d. being kept by the Association to make the boy a life member.

When Hugill left in 1961, and Holden became temporary Headmaster he approached the Association, and asked if members would be prepared to give advice on careers to boys in their last year at School. This was agreed to and meetings were held with those interested.

It was the custom for the photographs of Presidents to be hung in the School Hall, and there was also a board recording their names. At the request of Moody the photographs were taken down, and mounted in an album, but the photograph of the reigning President continued to be displayed.

In 1964 a badge of Office was provided for the President for the first time, but a much more important happening was the publication of the report of the Borough Education Officer – W. R. Tuson – *Organisation of Secondary Education – A reappraisal*, which sounded the death knell of the School. (For details of the proposals see Chapter 13.) The Association formed a Sub-Committee to consider the matter. The proposals were strongly opposed, and a press campaign was started in company with the Parent Teachers Association, the Park School P.T.A. and the Old Girls Association, and Moody. An attempt was made to get Tuson to address the Chamber of Commerce on the subject along with Moody, but he refused to do so if Moody was present. The Association members were particularly angered because Tuson was an Old Boy of the School (but not a member of the Association).

An anti-reorganisation meeting was held in the Public Hall, and Moody got up a petition. The result was that in March 1965 Tuson wrote to the Association stating that the scheme was to be deferred for twelve months so that national opinion could be sounded. The Association prided itself that, along with others, it had prevented a hasty step being taken. It later appeared that comprehensive education would be introduced, and that the Association had done all that it could to prevent it. It was therefore necessary to bow to the inevitable. In December 1968 the Notice of Intent to close the School was issued. The Association objected forcefully, but accepted that the objection was hopeless, and was merely a token.

Meanwhile there was concern about the rise of the Association's share in the cost of the *Hoghtonian*, and after some consideration it was decided to discontinue the Association's section, and to again publish a separate magazine. The first issue was in 1966, the second in December 1967, and the third, and last at Easter 1969.

In November 1969 the Association was very concerned when a boy sat on the case in the School Hall containing the Memorial Book, and broke the glass. Consideration was given to removing the Book, and it was ascertained that the Parish Church was prepared to receive it. A meeting was held with Tuson, who was very apologetic about the damage, and suggested that the Book should remain at the School until the new 6th form College was built, when a special place would be found for it there. This was agreed to, subject to a written undertaking being given that it would be properly looked after. It is noteworthy that the case was only repaired a year after the damage was done. The Book stayed at the School, but in 1972 the matter was again raised, and the President of the Association J. Brandwood, and W.G. Hunniball visited the School to discuss the Book with Miss Shanks the Principal of the College. They reported back to the Executive Council with a recommendation that the Book should remain at the School until the new College was ready, and then be moved there. A debate followed, and it was decided not to accept the recommendation, but to transfer the Book to the Parish Church. (It may be that the decision was made because it was then known that the new College was to be called the W. R. Tuson College.) There was strong opposition to this from the College staff, and the Association's representatives had to point out that the Book was the property of the Association. The Book was placed in the Church and there was a service of re-dedication in 1973. The 1914–18 plaque was also removed to the Church in 1982, and a grant of £250 was made by the Association. On 11 November 1984 a Remembrance Service was held in the Parish Church, attended by Old Boys and their wives. Since then a similar service has been held every year on the afternoon of Remembrance Sunday.

In 1973 there was also a proposal to remove the 'Tudor Window' (see Appendix II), to the Tuson College. This was strongly objected to, and did not take place. Other items were removed to the College without objection, and in 1979 it was suggested that the School's sporting trophies, which were stored in the muniment room at the Town Hall, should be offered to the College. In fact it appeared that no sports were being played at the College, and therefore no interest was expressed. The historical paintings that had been in the Hall of the School were removed, and were rehung in the Fulwood High School.

In 1980 the Association was approached with a proposal for the foundation of a new private Grammar School in Preston. It was a detailed scheme which would cater for 350 pupils of both sexes, and it was hoped to open in 1981. Nothing further seems to have been heard of the venture.

In 1989 the organ at the School was dismantled, and the Presidents' name-board was removed. Tuson College was renamed 'Preston College' at the same time.

In 1994 it was decided to commemorate the death of Ernest Walters, the oldest member of the Association, and one of the most active. He had deposited a large number of copies of the *Hoghtonian* in the Harris Reference Library before his death, and it was decided to complete the set, and have it bound in leather. With some difficulty H. W. L. Cumming managed to find the missing copies, and they were accordingly handsomely bound and, on 23 February 1995, were presented to The Right Worshipful the Mayor of Preston to be preserved in the Harris Reference Library.

Despite the disappearance of the School the Association has continued to flourish; there are over 300 members. The Annual Dinner is well attended, and the London Section, after a lapse some years ago, still carries on. In view of these activities it is most likely that the Association will continue into the next century.

Appendix I

Headmasters

1230	Willelm de Kirkham?
1358	John the clerk of Broghton
1399	Richard Marshall or le Marishall, clerk
1474	Thomas Preston, clerk
died 1518	George Hale, clerk
1518	Roger Levens or Lewyns, clerk
1548–61	Nicholas Banastre, clerk
1561–87	William Clayton
1587–90	Peter Carter MA St John's College, Cambridge
1602–07	William Gellibrand BA Brasenose College, Oxford
1607–16	Henry Yates
1616–36	Hugh Whalley
1636–49	Roger Sherburne
1650	William Robinson
1656	Mr Winckley
1662	William Yates (possibly usher)
1675	Richard Taylor
1675–77	William Barrowe MA Corpus Christi College, Oxford
1677–80	George Walmesley MA Jesus College, Cambridge
1680–89	Richard Croxton, or Croston BA Emmanuel College, Cambridge
1689	Thomas Whitehead BA Jesus College, Cambridge
1689–98	Thomas Lodge St Edmund's Hall, Oxford
1698–1704	Edward Denham MA Kings's College, Cambridge
1704–08	William Powell
1708–26	Edward Mainwaring St John's College, Cambridge
1726–37	William Davies MA Christ Church College, Oxford
1737–64	Rev. Robert Oliver MA Merton College, Oxford
1765–70	Ellis Henry BA Brasenose College, Oxford
1771–88	Thomas Fleetwood
1788–1835	Rev. Robert Harris BD Sidney Sussex College, Cambridge

1835–55	Rev. George Nun Smith MA Sidney Sussex College, Cambridge
1855–57	Rev. Edwin Smith MA St John's College, Cambridge
1857–58	Rev. John Richard Blakiston MA Trinity College, Cambridge
1859	Rev. John William Caldicott MA Jesus College, Oxford
1859–74	Rev. George Turner Tatham MA St John's College, Cambridge
1874–98	Rev. Alfred Beaven Beaven MA Pembroke College, Cambridge
1898–1911	Rev. Henry Cribb Brooks MA Trinity College, Dublin and St Catherine's College, Cambridge
1911	Rev. Francis Ernest Brown MA Hertford College, Oxford
1912–26	Rev. Norman Trewby MA Hertford College, Oxford
1926–47	Norman Hodgson MA Queen's College, Oxford
1947–48	Frederick Kite Dodson MA Downing College, Cambridge (acting)
1948–57	Eric Johnson MA Peterhouse College, Cambridge
1957–61	Michael James Hugill MA King's College, Cambridge
1961–62	Fred Pickup Holden MA, Emmanuel College, Cambridge (acting)
1962–66	Bernard John Moody MA, FRIC, St John's College, Cambridge
1966–69	Fred Pickup Holden and J. D. Warburton MA Queen's College, Cambridge (acting)

Appendix II

Roll of Honour, 1914–1918

J. E. B. Adkins

R. Bannister

G. Bott

W. E. B. Burton (Assistant Master)

P. Cumpstey

S. Dunwoody

H. Fazackerley

A. E. Hague

F. Hemsworth

R. T. W. Howe

C. W. Kay

E. Lomax

L. Metcalfe

M. Newhouse

C. E. Parkinson

F. Pomfret

A. E. Rawsthorn

N. O. Rigby

J. W. Shepherd

A. Snelham

A. Tullis

J. E. Whitehead

G. Woods

H. W. Allan

N. Bramwell

F. Brown

H. C. Crozier

A. Drysdale

Ll. F. Edwards

G. F. Glaister

A. N. Hargreaves

A. L. Howard

J. H. Jump

J. T. Livesey

F. Lucas

K. H. Moore

J. Parker

C. Pomfret

H. C. Rain

D. Reid

J. Robinson

P. T. Smith

P. Thexton

S. Ware

C. Whittle

Roll of Honour, 1939–1945

Royal Navy
Frederick Baines
Colin Birkett Bunce
Norman Lucas
Peter Royston Phillips

Harry Rainford
Thomas Edward Waud
Douglas Royland Webster
James Yates

Fleet Air Arm
John Arthur Seed

Fred Sumner

Royal Tank Regiment
Roland Henry Brown

Royal Armoured Corps
Brian Chandos Kirby

Northamptonshire Yeomanry
Abel Austin Roberts

Royal Regiment of Artillery
James Walmsley Ainsworth
John Hodson
Arthur Kempster

James Leslie Muir
Thomas Nash
George Telford Stevenson

Corps of Royal Engineers
Peter Woodhouse Smith

Royal Corps of Signals
Kenneth Walter Hill

William Midgley Robinson

The Loyal Regiment
Norman Parkinson

Kenneth Place

The Gordon Highlanders
George Herbert Worsley

Army Air Corps
David Fisher Kerr   Gordon Knight Richardson

Parachute Regiment
Alfred Hughes

Royal Army Service Corps
Frederick James Cater

Royal Army Medical Corps
Richard Kenneth Shaw

Army Dental Corps
Stanley Walch Gee   Hugh Heald

Royal Air Force
Robert Askew   Frederick Jackson Kemp
James Arthur Barnes   John Colin Marland
Fred Booth   William Marsden
Frank Bertram Brandwood   Kenneth Hunton Park
Eric Brindle   John Martland Parr
Raymond Culshaw   Walter Dennis Ramsay
James Robert Dobson   Edward Henry Ridgewell
Jack Burton Drury   John Frederick Sharples
Donald Antony Gee   William Cecil Smirk
Fred Gorst   Guy Benjamin Treasure
Thomas Griffith   John Preston Trewby
George Harris   Claude William Valder
Francis Helm   James Whalley
Ronald Denis Hilton   Geoffrey Prater Wilkinson
Ronald Lewis Howarth   Hubert Roy Wilmore
Alan Hewitt Abbott Johnson

Royal Canadian Air Force
Clifford MacKenzie Martin

Royal Air Force Regiment
William Arden Hogg   James Ronald Parker

Merchant Navy
Robert Carruthers Coulthard   Donald Reginald Noy

Appendix III

Presidents of the Association

Sir William Ascroft	1908–10
Sir George Toulmin	1910–12
Sir Robert Charles Brown	1912–25
J. M. Worthington	1925–27
H. P. Bee	1927–29
T. H. C. Derham	1929–31
W. H. Pimblett	1931–33
F. Friedenthal	1933–35
W. Rigby	1935–37
W. Smirk	1937–39
J. W. Taylor	1939–41
E. W. Wells	1941–43
E. Walters	1943–45
W. C. Attwater	1945–47
A. Winter	1947–49
J. Page	1949–51
F. K. Dodson	1951–53
W. G. Hunniball	1953–55
W. T. Broadbent	1955–57
M. Bagot	1957–58
J. M. Briggs	1958–59
F. Hind	1959–61
A. E. Willmoth	1961–63
A. W. Dawson	1963–65
G. Smithies	1965–67
F. Whittall	1967–69
A. R. W. Jones	1969–71
T. Heaps	1971–72
J. Brandwood	1972–73
C. E. Rigby MBE	1973–74
H. W. L. Cumming	1974–75
J. C. Turner	1976–77
W. Whalley	1977–78
M. Johnson	1978–79
R. E. Severs	1979–80

W. E. Mason	1980–81
C. Kay MBE	1981–82
F. W. Woodruff MBE	1982–83
C. Williams	1983–84
R. Sunderland	1984–85
J. R. Greenhalgh	1985–86
J. H. Taylor	1986–87
S. Rawlinson	1987–88
P. Ainscough	1988–89
J. Hamilton	1989–90
H. Barnett	1990
J. S. Treasure OBE	1990–92
H. H. Andrew	1992–93
D. C. Bunting	1993–94
K. W. Nightingale	1994–95
L. A. Pickston	1995–96

Appendix IV

Preston Grammar School Association Executive Council, 1995–1996

Ex Officio Members
The President — L. A. Pickston
Past Presidents
The Honorary General Secretary — G. Payne
The Honorary Treasurer — C. Foster

Elective Members
J. A. M. Bell
C. W. Bennett
J. R. M. Heppell

A. S. B. Olivine
J. B. S. Rigby
A. D. Varley

Appendix V

The Founder's Prayer

We give thee humble and hearty thanks, O most merciful Father, for our Founder, and all other our benefactors, by whose benefits we are, in this School brought up to godliness and good learning; and we beseech Thee to give us grace so to use these Thy blessings, to the glory of Thy Name so that we may become profitable members in the Church and Commonwealth, and may be at last partakers of the immortal glory of the Resurrection, through Jesus Christ, our Lord, Amen.

The Prefects' Declaration

I, being raised to the office, and authority of a Prefect over the boys of Preston Grammar School, with all its privileges, and responsibilities, do hereby promise, God helping me, strenuously to endeavour myself, so long as my office shall be retained:

1. To keep in the letter, and in the spirit, all the rules, regulations, unwritten laws, and traditions of Preston Grammar School.

2. To persuade, to help, and, with all those means lawfully within my power, to compel all boys to do the same.

3. Jealously to guard the good name, honour, and welfare of the School, to promote its efficiency, and to advance its interests whenever, and however it shall be possible.

4. Immediately bring to the notice of the Headmaster, or some other responsible authority, any matter, offence, or danger of evil beyond the reach of my own authority which might result in injury to the highest interests of the School.

5. To champion the interests and lawful privileges of the boys in the School; to protect the weaker and younger against oppression; to neglect no claim for help or sympathy; to see that justice is done, and to maintain the tradition of fair play.

6. To perform punctually, and conscientiously such duties as may be allotted to me.

If I find myself unable to fulfil this my promise of strenuous endeavour, God helping me, to carry out these duties, I engage to resign into the Headmaster's hands this my office and authority as a Prefect.

Appendix VI

The 'Tudor' Window

In the corridor behind the main door of the School building is a stained glass window consisting of three lights divided by stone mullions. It was moved from the Cross Street building to the Moor Park building in 1913. The history of this window, which appears to be very old, has puzzled many – Hodgson in 1939 wrote, in an introduction to an article that I wrote for the *Hoghtonian* on the Cuerdale Hoard, 'Research into the past history of the School might provide interesting results. The results of such enquiries hitherto are very meagre. What, for example, is the history of the stained glass in the entrance corridor? The significance of the design at least might be elucidated for us, and expert opinion obtained about the age of the plan'. About a year later an article was published in the *Hoghtonian*. It contained a careful description of the window by the Art Master H. Ogle:

The stained glass window of three lights, now boarded up, opposite to the Headmaster's study door is an original work of the sixteenth century. Its period is Tudor, but it is for the expert in heraldry and glass painting to decide whether it was painted in the reign of Henry VIII, Edward VI, or Queen Elizabeth.

The window was designed as a complete royal armorial decoration; that is to say, a shield of arms surmounted by a crown and encircled by the Garter, and with supporters right and left.

The supporter of the dexter, or right hand side of the shield (but on the left as you look at it) is a Lion *rampant* for England, bearing a banner with the combined York and Lancaster Rose, red and white on a blue field. The Supporter on the sinister side is a Griffin *segreant* for Wales, bearing a banner with a portcullis, gold on a blue field. The portcullis was the device of Lady Margaret Beaufort, mother of Henry VII. '*Segreant*' is an heraldic term for 'having the wings upraised as though about to fly'.

In the Middle light is a Royal Shield of Arms encircled by the Garter, which bears the motto 'Honi soit qui mal y pense', partly hidden by the overlapping parts of the ornate shield. The buckle and end of the Garter can be seen below the shield. The shield is divided quarterly, with the three lilies or *fleurs de lis* of France and the three lions of England, both emblems gold, the lilies on a blue field and the lions on a red. The immediate background of both is black, devised by the craftsman to make the lilies and lions to stand out clearly, and not intended by the designer to be a heraldic 'colour'. In our window two of the lions are upside-down – either abysmal ignorance or '*lèse majeste*', on the part of the modern restorer.

Above the shield is the Royal Crown (of two arches crossing at right angles in the actual object itself as distinct from the painting of it). The arches of the crown meet on a ball bearing a cross. We see one 'end-on' the ball and cross at the top and a cross at the bottom. The arches spring from a circle of crosses and lilies, with a band of jewels below it.

The background of the whole composition is made up of firstly, at the top Lancaster Roses, red on a green field, secondly, diagonal bands of Gothic black lettering separated by bands of ornament in yellow 'silver stain', thirdly, in the case of the supporters, grass and flowers in green. In the middle light are York and Lancaster Roses below the Crown and below the Garter. The diagonal bands bear the motto '*Dieu et Mon Droit*', that of the Sovereign.

Study of the glass itself, as distinct from the study of a photograph reveals the fact that the lilies are surrounded by black 'quarries' surrounded by the blue of the field. This should dispose of the suggestion that the lilies were intended as a device upon a pallium, which is an ecclesiastical vestment of capital Y shape worn over the shoulders with one part hanging down in front. When three lilies were shown they were usually placed as here, two over one. As a work of art the window is a first-rate example of its period, just when decadence both in heraldry and in glass painting began. The emblems and supporters admirably fill their appointed spaces, the drawing is vigorous and powerful, and the colour rich and varied. Signs of the decadence to come are apparent in the attempt at naturalism in the supporters. The heraldic lion should be an imaginary rather than a menagerie beast. The brushwork and sparing use of fussy shading show artistic insight such as is seldom found today.

The article was probably written because the window had been inspected and photographed by the Record and Survey Committee of the Preston Scientific Society, under its Chairman J. H. Spencer. No doubt the record of the window was made because of the danger of damage to it as a result of the War. As mentioned in Ogle's note it had been boarded up to protect it from the possibility of bomb damage. Spencer also described it for '*Notes and Queries*', and there were two comments as a result, which did not take the matter any further (see vol. 178, pp. 315, 357 and 377).

Comments were also received from A. J. Hawkes, the Borough Librarian of Wigan. It was he who mentioned the 'pallium' which Ogle refers to. The reason for this is that in the black and white photograph it does appear that the *fleur de lis* are on a capital V. In fact no such V appears on the window, but the blue glass upon which the *fleur de lis* appear is shaded and gives this effect in a black and white, but not in a colour photograph. Hawkes went on to consider the date of the foundation of the School, but his views on that have no relevance.

The Vicar of Preston, Canon Wallis, also gave his opinion, including a suggestion that the window might have been moved from the Parish Church when it was rebuilt in the nineteenth century.

There the matter rested until 1973 when it was proposed to move the window to Tuson College. This was strongly opposed by the Association, and did not take place. In 1975 the County Council suggested moving the window to a new and safer position. The Borough Council objected, and said that, if it was to be moved, it should go to the Museum. At that time it was stated that it was worth about £500,000. This caused S. Sartin, the then Assistant Keeper of Arts at the Harris Museum to carefully examine the window. His discoveries were reported in the *Lancashire Evening Post* on 8 November 1975.

Sartin noticed that the shield did not display the normal Royal Arms, since the three lions were in profile, and not facing the observer. It then appeared that a legend had grown up in the school about the window to the effect that it had come from Hampton Court, and that the arms were those of Henry VIII. How this legend originated I do not know. I certainly never heard it when at the School between 1932 and 1939. Hodgson did not know of it, nor did any of those involved in the *Hoghtonian* article of 1940, nor is it mentioned in any part of the *Hoghtonian*, which contains many stories and reminiscences of Old Boys. It therefore seems that it is a modern invention. Sartin considered that the window was designed by Thomas Willement who was employed by Ballantynes of Edinburgh who were manufacturers of stained glass windows. As is mentioned in Chapter 7 they were employed to put stained glass windows into the Cross Street School in 1845. They also provided the windows for the new Houses of Parliament in the 1840s, and, curiously enough, worked on stained glass windows at Hampton Court during the same period, and on those in Preston Parish Church. Sartin's researches certainly place grave doubts as to the antiquity of the window, but a doubt must remain as to its true history. Why are the lions looking forward? A Tudor artist would surely get it right, but then so would a Victorian designer of the standing of Willement. Why are two of the lions in the bottom quarter upside-down, as noted by Ogle? Furthermore an examination of a colour photograph shows that some of the glass seems to have been replaced, for example a large piece on the right flank of the supporting lion is of a different colour to the rest of the body, and has no detail painted on it, and a number of the pieces of blue glass are of a much lighter shade than the rest, and this is obviously not for any artistic reason. The window has therefore been renovated at some time, and not put together correctly (witness the upside-down lions). This could have been done at the time of the move to Moor Park, but it could have been done much earlier. Did Willement find the window somewhere (perhaps even at Hampton Court!), and, as it was eminently suitable for the School, furbish it up, and install it at Cross Street? We shall never know, but as a final point – if it was designed for Cross Street, why does it show the Royal Arms, and not the School arms? In other words, although the Rose and Portcullis are correct for the School, why are the arms of Preston not there, as they were, with the Rose and Portcullis, in the carving over the entrance to Cross Street?

Appendix VII

The Grammar School and Freemasonry

MANY OF THE OLD BOYS and Masters of the School were Freemasons, and, in May 1938, C. W. Rogers, the Chemistry Master wrote to a number of them suggesting that a meeting should be held to consider the formation of a School Lodge. The meeting was held, and it was resolved to proceed, but the outbreak of war in 1939 prevented any further steps being taken.

In August 1945 a further meeting was held, and it was decided that a Lodge should be formed, to be named 'The Preston Portcullis Lodge' which was to meet at the Bull and Royal Hotel.

The foundation of the Lodge was supported by the Association, although a few members were not in favour.

In May 1946 a Petition was signed by the 32 Founders, and presented to the Royal Preston Lodge No. 333, which was to act as sponsor. The Lodge was duly consecrated on 28 November 1946 at the Preston Masonic Temple. The first Master was J. M. Worthington who was Deputy to the Chancellor of the Duchy, and Registrar of the Chancery of Lancaster. The Lodge was numbered 6316. A Lodge Banner was designed by H. Ogle, the Art Master at the School, and it was decided that Association ties should be worn in Lodge instead of the customary black tie.

In 1950 the Lodge joined the Federation of School Lodges, and in 1964 a Royal Arch Chapter was formed.

When the old School at Cross Street was demolished in 1956 some stone from the building was obtained to make ashlars for the Lodge.

The Lodge has continued to flourish, but, owing to the closure of the School in 1969, applicants for membership began to fall off, and it therefore became necessary to open membership to those who are not former pupils of the School.

Perhaps one of the best known Masons, who was an Old Boy of the School, was Fred L. Pick, who attended at Cross Street and moved to Moor Park in 1913. He held many Masonic Offices, in particular he was a founder of the Manchester Lodge for Research, and a Master of the Quatuor Coronati Lodge. For a number of years he was Provincial Grand Secretary of the Province of East Lancashire. In 1953, in collaboration with G. Norman

Knight he published *The Pocket History of Freemasonary*, and, later *The Freemason's Pocket Reference Book*. The former book was a landmark in such works, and is still in print. He died in 1967.

Appendix VIII

The Caretakers

THERE were four caretakers employed at the School over a period of about 80 years, and all of them were not only excellent caretakers, but also friends of the boys.

Richard Leach

He was employed by the Corporation on 7 May 1883 to work at the Town Hall. Prior to this employment he had served in the Coldstream Guards. There was no caretaker at Cross Street at that time, only a woman cleaner. As she was growing old, Leach was deputed to assist her each evening, after his work at the Town Hall. About 1900 he became a full-time caretaker at Cross Street – the first that the School had ever had. He was known to the boys as 'Dick', and was very popular with them, despite his habit of eating the potatoes that they had surreptitiously put to roast before the heating furnace.

When the School moved to Moor Park Avenue he moved with it, and continued to work there until his retirement in 1918.

Jim Mills

The successor of Leach was Jim Mills who was employed from 1918 to 1936. He was a kindly man, much loved by the boys, but he had a great belief in discipline, and obedience to School rules. One evening he heard loud noises coming from the Detention Room, and on investigation found that there was no Master present. He then remembered seeing the Master, who should have been there, leaving the building, having forgotten that he was on duty. Jim took charge, and supervised the Detention Class until the appointed hour. He then released the boys, who ran in a crowd to get out of the building as fast as possible. He shouted to them that all the doors were locked, brought them back to the classroom, and made them march in single file to the door before he would let them out.

One of his joys was to take part in the performances of the School Orchestra, where he played the drums. He was very fond of telling stories of football in the good old days when the 'Old Invincibles' flourished, and he also remembered a great team of 'mule tenters' (i.e. men who looked after spinning mules) who played in bare feet.

Joseph Messenger

Jim was a difficult man to replace, but Joe Messenger, who started work in January 1937, became almost as popular. He was a small man, always with a twinkle in his eye, and and a worthy successor. Unfortunately he died suddenly in August 1945.

George T. Benson

Like Leach, Benson had been a regular soldier. He joined the East Lancashire Regiment in 1922, and served in Germany, Egypt and India. While stationed at Fulwood Barracks, before the War, he had given boxing lessons at the School, for he was a good middleweight boxer, which gave rise to his nick-name of 'Bash'.

During the War he served in Madagascar and Burma, and was demobilised in 1945, and at once took up duties at the School. In addition to his work as caretaker he became a Warrant Officer in the School's Air Training Corps Squadron, and was awarded the R. A. F. Cadet Force Medal.

Sources and Bibliography

THE OFFICIAL SOURCES for the history of the School are the Minutes of the Borough Council, and its Committees – the Grammar School Committee, the Board of Governors, and the Education Committee. These are contained in the Minute Books, the first of which is the 'White Book', or Book of Orders which covers the period from 1608 to 1758. This and the later Minute Books up to 1959 are in the County Record Office. The later Books are in the Preston Reference Library.

Also in the County Record Office, and in the Preston Reference Library are miscellaneous collections of documents relating to the School. There are also copy reports on scholars, and details of Masters and Mistresses.

The next most important source is the School Magazine, the *Hoghtonian*, which was published from December 1913 to July 1967. A complete set was bound by the Association, and presented to the Borough for deposit in the Preston Reference Library. The magazine was generally issued three times a year, and purports to be divided into 'volumes' up to December 1937, when this practice ceased. The system was very erratic, and reference is therefore best made to the year and month – there is no index.

The Association also published its own magazine from 1910 to 1914, and again from 1967 to 1969. Copies are in the Preston Reference Library. In 1925 an Association section was incorporated in the *Hoghtonian*. I have consulted the Minutes of the meetings of the Association from 1952, and also the Minutes of the meetings of the Parent/Teachers Association from 1964–1969.

There has never been a full history of the School. A person writing under the pseudonym 'Battleaxe' contributed four articles to the *Preston Herald* on 22 and 29 September, and 6 and 13 October 1894, containing something over 7,000 words. He ended with the appointment of Robert Harris as Headmaster in 1788. The History is detailed, and obviously owes a great deal to the 'White Book', but is inaccurate in some respects. The only other attempt at a history was the short note that Brooks prepared for a brochure that he issued. This was the basis for the notes in later brochures issued by Johnson and Hugill. An Outline History was also issued by the Association in the 1960s, and a *History of the Association* was published in 1953. There are numerous historical notes in the *Hoghtonian*.

For the details leading to the closure of the School I have had the great advantage of seeing a copy of a Dissertation entitled *Decision Making in English Education – A Case-Study of the Decision to Create a Tertiary College in Preston* by Ian B. Hoyle.

All the Histories of Preston give some details of the School, but the latest of these is Clemesha's published in 1912 (apart from Hunt's History which does not contain any mention of the School after the Great War), and there is therefore no help to be gained from them in respect of the period after 1918. For the earlier period they are most useful, particularly Leach's chapter in Volume Two of the *Victoria County History of Lancashire* and Fishwick's *History of the Parish of Preston*, both of which provide details of early Headmasters.

Books consulted

Baines, Edward, *History, Directory and Gazetteer of the County Palatine of Lancaster.* Volume 2 (1825).

——, *The History of the County Palatine and Duchy of Lancaster*, edited by J. Hereford, Volume 2 (1870).

——, As above, edited by J. Croston, Volume 5 (1893).

——, *Life of, by his son* (1851).

Berry, A. J. , *The Story of Preston* (1912).

——, *Proud Preston's Story* (1928).

Boyd, W., *The History of Western Education*, 8th edn (1966).

Briggs, J. M. , *The Preston Portcullis Lodge – The First Forty Years* (1986).

Brown, Sir Charles, *Sixty-four Years a Doctor* (1922).

Cartulary of Cockersands Abbey, Chetham Society, NS, volume 39.

Charity Commissioners, 'Report of the Commissioners to Enquire Concerning Charities' (1890).

Clemesha, W., *A History of Preston in Amounderness* (1912).

——, *Bibliography of the History of Preston*

Crosby, A., *The History of Preston Guild* (1991).

Dictionary of National Biography

Draper, P., *The House of Stanley* (1864).

Fishwick, Lt-Col., *History of the Parish of Preston* (1900).

Gastrell, Bishop F., *Notitia Cestriensis*, Chetham Society OS, Volume 22 (1850).

Hardwick, C., *History of the Borough of Preston* (1857).

Hewitson, A., *History of Preston* (1883).

——, *Preston Court Leet Records* (1905).

Holmes, Sir Charles, *Self and Partners (mostly Self)* (1936).

Howard, F., Paper presented to the Historical Society of Lancashire and Cheshire on paintings at Cross Street – Transactions, Volume I (1848).

Hoyle, Ian B., *Decision-Making in English Education A Case-Study of the Decision to Create a Tertiary College in Preston* (1977).

Hunt, D., *A History of Preston* (1992).

Leach, A. F., *English Schools at the Reformation 1546–48* (1896).

——, *The Schools of Medieval England* (1915).

MacKenzie, Sir Compton, *Aegean Memories* (1940).

Mark, E. N., *Guild guide to Preston* (1882).

Millar, R. *Kut – The Death of an Army* (1969).

Nabarro, Derrick, *Wait for the Dawn* (1952).

Pollard, W., *A Handbook and Guide to Preston* (1882).

Raines, Rev. F. R., *A History of the Chantries within the County Palatine of Lancaster, being the Reports of the Royal Commissions of Henry VIII, Edward VI and Queen Mary*, Volume 2, Chetham Society, OS, Volume 60 (1862).

Read, G. *Richard Arkwright – the Happy Mechanic* (1982).

Ryan, C., *A Bridge Too Far* (1974).

Sartin, S., *Historic Preston* (1988)

Smith, T. C., *Records of the Parish Church of Preston in Amounderness* (1892).

Victoria History of Lancashire, edited by W. Farrer and J. Brownbill, Volume 2 (1908): the chapter on grammar schools is by J. F. Leach.

Whittle, P. (sub. nom. Tulket, M.), *A Topographical, Statistical and Historical Account of the Borough of Preston* (1821).

——, *The History of the Borough of Preston* (1837).

Who's Who 1995.

Wilson, Rev. R., *Life of Peter Hoghton, BA* (1932)

Anonymous, *The History of Preston in Lancashire, with the Guild Merchant* (1822).

Notes

I HAVE NOT THOUGHT IT NECESSARY to include footnotes, or cover the pages with small figures giving reference to the authority for each statement made. In particular I do not provide references to the minutes of the Council and its Committees because in each case the date of the resolution is given in the text. I do generally give references to the *Hoghtonian*, because there is no index to the bound volumes. The following are short notes upon some points of interest.

Chapter 1 – The Medieval Period

The Victoria County History, Volume II, p. 569 *et seq.* by A. F. Leech deals with the theory that the School existed in 1230. Cartulary of Cockersands Abbey is in Chetham Society, NS, Volume 39, p. 217.

Fishwick p. 204 states that the name of the schoolmaster of Preston prosecuted in 1358 is not known. The list of those charged include John le Clerk de Broghton, and following this name the words 'Magister, the schoolmaster of Preston'. Fishwick assumes that these are two distinct persons, the latter not named. I follow Leech (op. cit.) in not agreeing with Fishwick.

N. B. Fishwick is very useful, but Clemesha in his *Bibliography of the History of Preston* points out that it is not safe to accept statements by him without verification.

Chapter 2 – The Hoghton Chantry

For details of the Chantry, and its history see Chetham Society, OS, Volume 60, pp. 205–207, and Smith's *Records of the Parish Church of Preston in Amounderness* pp. 230–233.

Chapter 3 – Elizabeth I to the Restoration

Peter Carter is mentioned in the *Dictionary of National Biography*.
Details of the method of paying the Schoolmaster are in the 'White Book'.

Chapter 4 – 1660–1700

Worthington's Will is in the County Record Office. His troubles with his midden and land slips are mentioned in Hewitson's *Court Leet Records*
Kuerden's description is quoted in Hunt's *History of Preston*, p. 70.
Bishop Gastrell's *Notitia Cestriensis* is in Chetham Society, OS, Volume 22, p. 464. The Corporation's Rules for the School are in the 'White Book'.

Chapter 5 — 1704–1778

Details of the Council's problems with Headmasters are in the 'White Book'. Arkwright's activities at the Headmaster's House are mentioned in Read's *Richard Arkwright – the Happy Mechanic*, and in the Histories quoted in the text. The details of the election inquiry are in the County Record Office.

Robert Harris

See the Minutes for the troubles with Harris.
The *Charity Commissioners Report* was published in 1890 – copy in County Record Office.
Oakey's letter to Brooks is also in the County Record Office.

Chapter 7 — The Move to Cross Street

I have been unable to trace a copy of *The Scholar*. It is described in the *Hoghtonian* for December 1930 p. 304, and for December 1932 p. 239, so that at least one copy must have survived until then.

Chapter 9 — Beaven Beaven

Sir Charles Holmes' reminiscences are quoted in the *Hoghtonian* for December 1936 p. 142 from his Autobiography *Self and Partners (mostly Self)*.
Beaven's prospectus is in the County Record Office.
Hodgson's note on Beaven is in the *Hoghtonian* for December 1939, p. 13.

Chapter 10 — H. C. Brooks

Brooks' letter to parents, and the Town Clerk's letter to Brooks are in the County Record Office, as are Brooks' prospectus, and instructions for dress in the Guild Procession.
Martin's reminiscences are in the *Hoghtonian* for Midsummer 1944, p. 3.
Letter from Brown in 1930 – see *Hoghtonian* for April 1930, p. 197

Chapter 11 — N. Trewby

The description of the organ is in the *Hoghtonian* for December 1913, p. 9, and the opening ceremony is described on pp. 2–6. Dr Sir Charles Brown wrote an autobiography – *Sixty Years a Doctor*.
The stories of Sinclair and Jackson are in the *Hoghtonian* for September 1914, pp. 70, 76.
The *Hoghtonian* carried notes of Masters and Old Boys in the Services throughout the War.
Details of the Memorial Window are in the *Hoghtonian* for July 1925, p. 5.
Copies of Trewby's prospectus are in the County Record Office.

Chapter 12 — Norman Hodgson

Details of the children adopted by the School are in the *Hoghtonian* for November 1927, p. 119.

For details of the School Parliament see the *Hoghtonian* for 1932 to 1934.

Annual School Camps are described in the *Hoghtonian*

Details of the effect of the outbreak of the War in September 1939 are in the *Hoghtonian* for December 1939, p. 15.

Derrick Nabarro D.C.M – see his own (somewhat novelised) account in his book *Wait for the Dawn*.

Crawley brothers – see obituary of Norman in the *Daily Telegraph* for 2 July 1990, and of Douglas in the *Lancashire Lad* for October 1986. Douglas is also mentioned in *A Bridge Too Far* by C. Ryan, 1974.

Details of the Memorial Book are in the *Hoghtonian* for January 1954, p. 55.

Chapter 13 – The Last Years

For this period it is necessary to consult the various reports prepared by the Borough Education Officer. Copies of the important ones are in the County Record Office. The Council and Committee minutes are in the Preston Reference Library. The best account of the negotiations leading to the implementation of the changes in Secondary Education is in Ian B. Hoyle's *Dissertation* (see Sources and Bibliography). I have also consulted the Minutes of the P.T.A., and the Association.

Chapter 14 – Arms, Mottos and Dress

The reference to Portcullis Pursuivant is in the *Hoghtonian* for December 1925, p. 18.

Chapter 15 – Scholarships and Prizes

Details of Goodair, Miller and Harris are in Hunt's *History of Preston*.

Chapter 16 – Sports

The *Hoghtonian* contains many details of both inter-house, and inter-school sport. See the Council Minutes for details of playing fields, and the pavilion.

Chapter 17 – Some Famous Old Boys

Edward Stanley – see *The House of Stanley* by P. Draper. Mention of his being at the School is in the *Hoghtonian* for December 1913, p. 5.

The story of Danson is in the *Hoghtonian* for March 1937, p. 8.

Edward Baines – see the *Life* by his son.

Sir Percy Lake – see the *Dictionary of National Biography* and 'Kut – The Death of an Army' by R. Millar, 1969.

Sir John Myers – see *Dictionary of National Biography* and 'Aegean Memories' by Sir Compton MacKenzie, 1940.

Mohamed Mahdi al-Tajir – see Profile in *Sunday Times* for 28 January 1990, p. C2, and *Who's Who* for 1995.

Chapter 18 – The Preston Grammar School Association

A short history of the *Association* was privately published in 1953. A bound copy of the *Association* magazine published from 1910 to 1914 and copies from 1966 to 1969 are in the Preston Reference Library. I have also referred to the Minutes of the Council of the Association, and of the Annual General Meetings for 1952 to date (earlier Minute Books are not available).

Appendix V

Copies are in the County Record Office.

Appendix VI

See *Hoghtonian* for December 1940, p. 4, the Association Minutes, and the *Lancashire Evening Post* for 5 July and 8 November 1975.

Appendix VII

See *The Preston Portcullis Lodge – the First Forty Years* by J. M. Briggs. For Fred L. Pick see obituary in the *Association Magazine* for December 1967.

Appendix VIII

Details are in the *Hoghtonian* for January 1915, p. 97, December 1936, p. 148, Xmas 1945, pp. 4 and 9, and February 1964, p. 3. The story of the detention class was told to me by Jim himself.

List of Subscribers

The arrangements for the publication of this book required the Executive Council of the Preston Grammar School Association to agree to purchase a certain number of copies. In order to finance this requirement the Council invited members of the Association, and other interested persons to order and pay for copies in advance. The following is a list of those who did so, either in their own names, or in the names of deceased members, and others. They thereby ensured that the publication of this book could proceed.

Adams T. E. (deceased)
Ainscough P.
Airey J. E.
Aldington P. J.
Allan H. R.
Andrew H. H.
Andrew S. R.
Armstrong H. M.
Ashcroft J.
Bamber J. F.
Bamber M. P.
Banks A. G.
Beaumont A.
Bell D.
Bell J. A. M.
Bennett C. W.
Billington D. (C)
Blackburn W. E. (deceased)
Bland J. M.
Bleasedale K. D.
Bleasedale W. J.
Bolton D. C.
Bomont R. G.
Bond F.
Booth B. G.
Booth G. (deceased)
Booth R. A.
Bramley J. G.
Brandwood F. B. (deceased)
Brandwood J.
Brennand J.
Brindle A. W.
Brindle J. (deceased)

Brown J.
Brunt D. A.
Bunting D. C.
Burrow R. G.
Caley I. F.
Carefoot C. M. J.
Caster A. C.
Challen R. D.
Clare R. D.
Clarke G. W.
Clarke P. B.
Clement R. B.
Connell G. W.
Cooper W. I.
Corner E.
Coulthard R. M.
Coulthurst F.
Cowperthwaite E.
Cowperthwaite I.
Craston D. M.
Craston R. C.
Cronkshaw H.
Crook R.
Cuerden I.
Cumming G. S.
Cumming H. W. D.
Cumming H. W. L.
Cunliffe L.
Dagger T.
Davies A. L.
Davy G. C.
Dawson A. W. (deceased)
Dawson W. F.

Dempsey J. P.
Dickson E. C.
Donkin L. J.
Dumbill A.
Durigan F. W.
Duxbury C.
Eccles L. R.
Eccles P. J.
Eccles R.
Ellwood G.
Emery D. J.
Emery J. H. (deceased)
Ennis R. B.
Facer A. S.
Facer M.
Fairclough W. D.
Fazackerley N.
Featherstone T. A.
Finch S. J.
Fisher A. C.
Foster C.
Foster J. C.
Freeman P. J.
Freeman W. (deceased)
Friedenthal G. L.
Gardner P. A.
Gillibrand S.
Gilroy D.
Goring G.
Goring J.
Gorton K. J.
Gorton M. H.
Grange J. G.

Greenhalgh J. R.
Greenhalgh M. J.
Greenhalgh W. N.
Hadwen F. A.
Hall B. J.
Halsall D.
Hamilton J.
Handley S. G.
Hayes G. E.
Heaton J.
Heaton J.
Heppell D. H.
Hesketh H. R.
Hesketh R. W.
Heywood T.
Hilton T. D.
Hodgson N. (deceased)
Holmes J. R.
Holmes L. H.
Hooley P. W.
Hornby R. B.
Houlder D.
Hoyle W.
Hugill M. J.
Insley J.
Jackson A.
Jackson D.
Jackson F.
Jepson H.
Johnson D.
Johnson D. V. Jnr.
Johnson J.
Johnson M.
Johnson S. F.
Johnstone H.
Jones A. R. W.
Jones F. D.
Kay C.
King E.
King M. R. (deceased)
Kirby W. S.
Lambert N. (deceased)
Leeming J. F.
Line G. W.
Martin G. W. (deceased)
McDowell J. M.
McGavin K. A.
McGunnigle P.
McTaggart S. H.

McWilliam D.
Mears D. M.
Mercer A. K.
Metcalf C.
Miller M.
Mills E. J.
Millward J.
Millward R.
Moody, B. J.
Murray I. N.
Myerscough P. R.
Nightingale K.
Nightingale K. W.
Noon G.
Oakley D. P.
Olivine A. S. B.
Owens E. E. L.
Owens G. L. (deceased)
Page J. T.
Parker L.
Parker T.
Payne G.
Pearson M.
Pearson R. J.
Pickston L. A.
Picton T. J.
Pinder J. H.
Pugh R. H.
Rance F. S.
Rance S. T.
Reed G. P.
Relph D. E. F.
Renwick J.
Richardson A.
Richardson J. W.
Richmond C. C.
Riseley R. B.
Roberts B. H.
Robertson W. M.
Robinson B. E.
Robinson R. I.
Robinson W. H.
Roulston D. R.
Round J. K.
Ryan W. E. D.
Saunders A.
Scott M. C.
Scott N. K.
Seed J. H.

Severs R. E.
Sharp D. J.
Simpson A. G.
Simpson J. D.
Simpson R. D.
Simpson R. J.
Singleton G. (deceased)
Sumner A.
Sunderland H.
Sunderland R.
Taylor D. L.
Taylor K. C.
Taylor R.
Thomas R. H.
Thompson A. G.
Thompson B. J.
Treasure F.
Treasure J. S.
Turner A. L.
Turner F. P.
Turner J. R.
Tyrer M. F.
Varley A. D.
Varley D. A.
Waddilove W. A.
Wade R. B.
Wall J. H.
Wallace J. C.
Walsh H.
Walsh R.
Walters E. (deceased)
Washington E. S.
Watson R. S.
Welch G.
Wells R. C.
Whalley H.
Whalley J. M.
Whalley K.
Whalley S. G.
Whiteside I.
Williams C.
Wilson D.
Wilson L.
Winwood H. C.
Withnell M. T.
Worthington G. W.
Young R.